Sanjeev Kapoor

100 Mouthwatering Recipes

In association with Alyona Kapoor

PopulaR prakashan

www.popularprakashan.com

Published by
POPULAR PRAKASHAN PVT. LTD.
301, Mahalaxmi Chambers
22, Bhulabhai Desai Road
Mumbai – 400 026
for KHANA KHAZANA PUBLICATIONS PVT. LTD.

© 2016 Sanjeev Kapoor
First Published 2016

(4427)
ISBN 978-81-7991-868-5

Design: Anjali Sawant

Printed in India
by Thomson Press (India) Ltd.
New Delhi

Author's Note

To shortlist just 100 mouthwatering Indian recipes is not an easy task, more so when one has spent over 30 years cooking and tasting hundreds and thousands of delicious recipes. Honestly, I find almost all of them to be delectable. However, in this book, I have managed to list 100 recipes that I think are really mouthwatering.

Indians love to entertain, and a scrumptious menu is top priority while entertaining the guests. We think good food, we talk good food and we love to serve and savour good food.

I have to say, having travelled all over the world, I have had the opportunity to taste the food that each country has to offer. They are all very good but, I take pride when I say that nothing compares to our very own Indian fare.

As you go through *100 Mouthwatering Recipes*, you will find each recipe to be very different from the other. All of them are simple and easy to cook with ingredients and spices that are easily available. The medley of herbs and condiments that give Indian food its identity are the mainstay of our preparations. Just a pinch of this and a dash of that and you have a delectable, lip-smacking, preparation ready to be served.

All the recipes serve four portions. They have been portioned thus with the idea that they form a part of a menu serving other complimentary dishes. I would like to add here that there are many more such recipes that I love to cook and serve. Maybe a few more such editions will do justice to our extensive repertoire.

This cookbook is written in an easy step-by-step method to help even a novice cook up a delicious meal. I am sure you will enjoy cooking them just as much as I enjoyed putting them together for you. So go ahead and indulge yourselves and your loved ones with an unforgettable spread.

Happy Cooking!

Contents

Chapter 1
Beverages, Soups and Salads

1 Imli Ka Amlana

Scorching summers? Worry not! This super-refreshing drink made with tamarind and just the right amount of spices will soothe your body at once. And then, you will not stop at one glass...

INGREDIENTS

4 tablespoons Tamarind Pulp (page 158)

1½ teaspoons black salt

⅓ teaspoon black pepper powder

⅓ teaspoon green cardamom powder

1 teaspoon Roasted Cumin Powder (page 158)

3 teaspoons roasted carom seed powder

6 tablespoons sugar

salt to taste

8-10 fresh mint leaves, roughly chopped

METHOD

- Add five cups of water to the tamarind pulp and mix well.

- Grind together the black salt, pepper powder, cardamom powder, cumin powder, carom seed powder, sugar and salt to a very fine powder.

- Add the mixture to the tamarind water and mix well. Chill in a refrigerator.

- Pour into Old-Fashioned glasses, decorate with fresh mint leaves and serve chilled.

2 Aam Ki Lassi

Mango milk shake is something that is taken for granted and is ever so popular. Why not do something more with luscious mango and make a lassi, that too with chocolate sauce!

INGREDIENTS

1 cup mango pulp

¼ cup sugar

3 cups yogurt

Crushed ice, as required

¼ cup chocolate sauce

15-20 pistachios, blanched and slivered

METHOD

- Transfer mango pulp into a blender.

- Add sugar and blend. Add yogurt and blend again. Add crushed ice and blend to a smooth mixture.

- Pour chocolate sauce in a squeezy bottle.

- Squeeze the sauce on the inner sides of the serving glasses in stripes.

- Pour lassi and fill up the glasses.

- Garnish with some more chocolate sauce and top with pistachio slivers and chocolate.

- Serve chilled.

3 Mixed Vegetable Soup

Add butter and lightly sauté nutritious veggies in a pan. Make this for the kids at home and your woes of feeding them healthy yet different food shall vanish at once! Kids will love it for sure!

INGREDIENTS

1 medium carrot, finely chopped

¼ medium cabbage, finely chopped

1 medium potato, finely chopped

2 medium tomatoes, finely chopped

1 tablespoon butter

1 medium onion, finely chopped

1 tablespoon whole-wheat flour

Salt to taste

Black pepper powder to taste

METHOD

- Heat the butter in a deep non-stick pan and sauté the onion till translucent.

- Add the chopped carrot, cabbage, potato and tomatoes, and stir to mix.

- Add the flour and cook, stirring, on medium heat for one or two minutes.

- Add the salt, pepper powder and four cups of water, and bring the mixture to a boil.

- Lower the heat and simmer for five to seven minutes, or till all the vegetables are cooked. Serve piping hot.

4 Gajar Shorba With Crisp Spinach And Toasted Sesame

Thick smooth carrot soup in its pink glory set up in juxtaposition with the green of fried spinach! That's a garnish with a real difference...

INGREDIENTS

5 medium carrots, grated

2 cups fresh spinach leaves, shredded

4 teaspoons sesame seeds, toasted

1 tablespoon butter

1 teaspoon cumin seeds

4 garlic cloves, chopped

1 inch ginger, chopped

4 cups Vegetable Stock (page 158)

1 medium potato, boiled and mashed

10-12 black peppercorns, crushed

Salt to taste

Oil for deep-frying

METHOD

- Heat the butter in a non-stick pan.

- Add cumin seeds and when they begin to change colour add garlic, ginger and carrots.

- Add one cup vegetable stock and cook till the carrots are soft. Remove from heat, cool and purée.

- Pour the purée into a deep non-stick pan.

- Add mashed potato, remaining stock, crushed peppercorns and salt.

- Cook, stirring continuously, till soup comes to a boil and is well blended. Pass the soup through a strainer.

- To make crisp spinach, heat sufficient oil in a non-stick kadai. Add the spinach and deep-fry till crisp. Drain.

- Pour the soup into individual bowls, garnish with crisp spinach and sprinkle toasted sesame seeds. Serve immediately.

5 Spinach Soup

When the emerald green spinach is perfectly spiced and simmered with milk to give a luscious and hearty soup. Looks great, tastes even better! Serves as a good option for lunch or dinner as well.

INGREDIENTS

1 kilogram spinach, roughly chopped

1 medium onion, chopped

1 tablespoon oil

1 bay leaf

6-8 black peppercorns

5 garlic cloves, chopped

3 cups Vegetable Stock (page 158) or water

½ teaspoon cumin powder

Salt to taste

½ teaspoon white pepper powder

1 cup milk

METHOD

- Heat the oil in a non-stick pan; add the bay leaf, peppercorns and chopped garlic. Stir-fry for half a minute.

- Add the chopped onion and cook, stirring continuously until the onion turns soft and translucent.

- Add the chopped spinach and continue to cook for three to four minutes. Remove from the heat. Cool the mixture.

- Remove the bay leaf and purée the spinach mixture to a fine consistency in a blender.

- Bring the vegetable stock or water to a boil; add the spinach purée, cumin powder, salt and white pepper powder to taste.

- Mix well, lower the heat and simmer for a few minutes. Stir in the milk and simmer for two minutes. Serve hot.

6 Red Pumpkin Soup

Pumpkin with spices and seasoning pressure-cooked to perfection, and voila! This orange-hued thick and wholesome soup is ready to satiate those odd-hour food cravings. You can turn it into a party-food when you serve this soup in the shells of scooped out small red pumpkins, no bigger than the size of a coconut.

INGREDIENTS

1 kilogram red pumpkin, diced

4 tablespoons butter

3 bay leaves

15-20 black peppercorns

3 large onions, sliced

4 cups Vegetable Stock (page 158) or water

Salt to taste

1 teaspoon white pepper powder

1 tablespoon lemon juice

½ cup fresh cream

METHOD

- Heat the butter in a pressure cooker; add the bay leaves and peppercorns.

- Add the onions and sauté for two minutes.

- Add the diced pumpkin and sauté for half a minute. Add four cups of water and cook under pressure until pressure is released once (one whistle).

- Strain and reserve the stock. Remove the bay leaves and discard. Purée the vegetables.

- Add the reserved stock and one cup of water to the purée.

- Add the salt and white pepper powder and bring to a boil. Stir in the lemon juice.

- Serve hot, garnished with fresh cream.

7 Tamatar Basil Shorba

Hot tomato soup is a comfort food for many of us. But whenever you need
a refreshing change top it up with fresh pesto, resplendent with basil.

INGREDIENTS

6 medium tomatoes, chopped

7 garlic cloves

1 inch cinnamon stick

1 black cardamom

10-12 black peppercorns

1 tablespoon cumin seeds

2 whole dried red chillies

½ cup chopped fresh coriander stems

3-4 basil stems

1 teaspoon oil

½ teaspoon red chilli powder

2 tablespoons gram flour

½ tablespoon lemon juice

Pesto

6-8 fresh basil leaves

3 garlic cloves

4 cashew nuts

4 tablespoons oil

METHOD

- Place the tomatoes, garlic, cinnamon, cardamom, peppercorns, cumin seeds, red chillies, coriander stems, basil stems, five cups of water and oil in a deep non-stick pan and bring to a boil.

- Cook for ten to twelve minutes, stirring frequently. Add chilli powder and mix. Take pan off the heat and strain into another deep non-stick pan.

- Add one cup water and boil for five minutes.

- Roast gram flour in another non-stick pan for four to five minutes or till fragrant.

- Add half cup water and mix well. Add this to shorba and boil for five minutes.

- To make the pesto, grind together basil leaves, garlic and cashew nuts with oil to a smooth paste. Set aside.

- Add lemon juice to the shorba and mix.

- Serve hot garnished with pesto.

8 Bhuni Makai Ka Soup

This is my sister's favourite soup. As a child she could slurp up this wonderfully-flavourful soup without any fuss. And my mother would be happy because makai(corn) is nutrient-rich besides being ever so tasty. The initial roasting gives the soup a pronounced smoky flavour.

INGREDIENTS

2 cups corn kernels

2 tablespoons butter

2 medium green capsicums, roasted, peeled and chopped

4 cups Vegetable Stock (page 158)

Salt to taste

2 teaspoons lemon juice

2 teaspoons chopped fresh coriander

METHOD

- Dry-roast the corn kernels in a non-stick pan for five to six minutes.

- Heat the butter in a deep non-stick pan. Add the capsicums and sauté for two minutes.

- Add the roasted corn kernels and sauté for three to four minutes.

- Add the vegetable stock and salt and bring to a boil. Simmer for three to four minutes.

- Take the pan off the heat and allow the contents to cool.

- Blend coarsely with a hand blender.

- Add the lemon juice, stir and bring the soup to a boil.

- Serve hot garnished with the chopped coriander.

9 Chicken Shorba

This rich Indian soup is definitely shahi with all the chicken and flavourful spices. Perfect for those chilly winter evenings when all you need is a bowlful of piping hot soup that does wonders to the body!

INGREDIENTS

500 grams chicken bones

100 grams boneless chicken, cut into ½-inch cubes

1 medium onion, roughly chopped

1 medium carrot, roughly chopped

1 bay leaf

4 black peppercorns

2 cloves

1 black cardamom

4 green cardamoms

1 inch cinnamon stick

2 tablespoons butter at room temperature

2 tablespoons refined flour

1 tablespoon oil

½ teaspoon cumin seeds

1 teaspoon crushed fennel seeds

10 garlic cloves, chopped

½ teaspoon white pepper powder

Salt to taste

METHOD

- Clean and wash the chicken bones.

- Boil four-and-a-half cups of water in a deep non-stick pan on high heat. Add the chicken bones, onion, carrot, bay leaf, peppercorns, cloves, black cardamom, green cardamoms and cinnamon and bring the mixture to a boil again.

- Continue to boil for twenty minutes or till the water is reduced to two and a half cups. Strain and set the stock aside.

- Heat one tablespoon butter in another non-stick pan. When the butter melts, add the chicken pieces and sauté till they get cooked and become tender. Drain and set aside.

- To make the roux, melt the remaining butter in the same pan. Add the flour and sauté for one to two minutes. Set aside.

- Heat the oil in another deep non-stick pan. Add the cumin seeds, fennel seeds and garlic. Sauté for one minute, lower heat to medium, add the roux, the reduced chicken stock, white pepper powder and salt.

- Cook, stirring continuously, and let the mixture come to a boil on high heat.

- Lower heat to medium, add the chicken pieces and simmer the soup for three to four minutes.

- Transfer into individual soup bowls and serve hot.

Chef's Tip: You may add half a cup of fresh cream just before serving to make it a little rich.

10 Paya Shorba (Lamb Trotter Soup)

If you are in Delhi in wintertime, you will be surprised by the carts that sprout up from nowhere to sell this! I am not sure which tastes better – the home version or the roadside version.

INGREDIENTS

10-12 lamb-trotters

4 medium onions

10 garlic cloves

½ teaspoon turmeric powder

6-8 cloves

4 green cardamoms

2 two-inch cinnamon sticks

Salt to taste

½ cup ghee

½ teaspoon red chilli powder

½ teaspoon black pepper powder

A small bunch of fresh coriander, chopped

1 teaspoon garam masala powder

1 tablespoon lemon juice

METHOD

- Scrub, clean and wash trotters thoroughly under running water and drain.

- Quarter two onions and finely slice the remaining. Grind the quartered onions with garlic to a paste.

- In a large non-stick deep pan add fifteen cups of water and trotters. Add onion-garlic paste, turmeric powder, cloves, green cardamoms, cinnamon and salt. Cook for four hours on low heat (dum) or till the trotters are tender. If required, add another two to three cups of water.

- Heat ghee in a non-stick pan and sauté sliced onions till golden brown. Add chilli powder and pepper powder. Add to trotters and cook for five minutes. Strain the liquid and separate the trotters from the residue.

- Heat the strained liquid with chopped coriander, garam masala powder and the trotters.

- Remove from heat when ghee rises to the surface. Add lemon juice.

- Serve with roti, phulka or sheermal.

11 Papad Koshimbir

This crunchy salad is a great appetiser. Remember to serve it immediately, before the papad turn soggy.

INGREDIENTS

6 masala papad, roasted

1 small onion, finely chopped

1 medium tomato, finely chopped

1 green chilli, finely chopped

2 tablespoons freshly grated coconut

2 teaspoons lemon juice

¼ teaspoon red chilli powder

Chaat Masala (page 156), to taste

Salt to taste

2 tablespoons finely chopped fresh coriander

METHOD

- Combine the onion, tomato, green chilli and coconut in a bowl and mix well.

- Add the lemon juice, chilli powder, chaat masala and salt and mix again. Crush the papad and add. Mix gently.

- Serve immediately, garnished with the chopped coriander.

12 Three Chilli Potato Salad

Don't get misled by the name - this dish is not all that spicy, since the 'chillies' refers to the capsicums of three different colours and not Kashmiri red chilli, peppercorns and chilli flakes. In fact, we initially had a tough time making our chefs understand that! It's so very delicious that I am often tempted to make a full meal of this salad. At our restaurants too it has caught on big time.

INGREDIENTS

32-34 baby potatoes, boiled and peeled

¾ teaspoon turmeric powder

1½ teaspoons red chilli powder

Salt to taste

1 teaspoon black pepper powder

2 tablespoons oil

1 medium red capsicum, thickly sliced

1 medium yellow capsicum, thickly sliced

1 medium green capsicum, thickly sliced

1 medium tomato, seeded and thickly sliced

1 medium onion, thickly sliced and layers separated

2 tablespoons tomato ketchup

½ tablespoon Tamarind Pulp (page 158)

1 teaspoon Chaat Masala (page 156)

1 tablespoon lemon juice

1 teaspoon crushed black peppercorns

1 sprig fresh coriander

1 lemon, cut into wedges

METHOD

- Preheat oven to 240⁰C/ 475⁰F/Gas Mark 9.

- Mix together turmeric powder, chilli powder, salt, pepper powder and oil.

- Apply this paste to the potatoes and place them in a baking tray and bake in the preheated oven for ten to fifteen minutes.

- Remove from the oven and set aside to cool.

- Transfer the potatoes into a bowl, add red capsicum, yellow capsicum, green capsicum, tomato and onion and mix well.

- Add tomato ketchup, tamarind pulp, chaat masala, salt, lemon juice and crushed black peppercorns and mix well.

- Serve garnished with coriander sprigs and lemon wedges.

13 **Chickpea** Salad

Chole is not the only thing that we can cook up with chickpeas or kabuli chane. In our refrigerator you will always find a lot of boiled kabuli chane so that we churn up some wonderful things with them in a jiffy. Wholesome and piquant, it is a salad but it can be had as an anytime snack.

INGREDIENTS

1½ cups chickpeas, soaked overnight and boiled till soft

2 small potatoes, boiled, peeled and cut into small cubes

2 small tomatoes, chopped

2 teaspoons chopped fresh coriander

1 green chilli, chopped

2-3 teaspoons lemon juice

¼ teaspoon black salt

Salt to taste

2 teaspoons Chaat Masala (page 156)

METHOD

- Mix together the boiled chickpeas, potatoes, tomatoes, chopped coriander, green chilli, lemon juice, black salt, salt and chaat masala in a large bowl.

- Toss all the ingredients well to mix.

- Serve immediately.

14 Five **Sprouts** Salad

Sprouted seeds, grains and pulses are rich sources of B vitamins. And they are a part of traditional cuisine in this country, adding taste, texture and nutrition to almost anything that they are part of. They are better eaten raw, but could set off allergies, so a light sauté with very little oil or blanching them will deal with that problem.

INGREDIENTS

¼ cup sprouted brown Bengal gram

¼ cup sprouted white peas

½ cup sprouted green gram

½ cup sprouted red lentil

½ cup sprouted brown gram

Salt to taste

1 medium tomato, finely chopped

1 medium onion, finely chopped

1 tablespoon lemon juice

Black salt to taste

1 teaspoon Chaat Masala (page 156)

½ teaspoon red chilli powder

½ cup crushed roasted peanuts

2 tablespoons chopped fresh coriander

METHOD

- Boil four cups of water in a deep non-stick pan. Add salt, brown Bengal gram and white peas and boil for ten to fifteen minutes.

- Add the green gram, red lentils and brown gram and continue to boil for seven to eight minutes more.

- Drain and transfer into a large bowl.

- Add the tomato, onion, lemon juice, black salt, chaat masala, chilli powder and peanuts and mix.

- Garnish with chopped coriander and serve immedietely.

15 Fruit And **Capsicum** Kachumber

Literally, a kachumber refers to an Indian salad consisting of a mix of seasoned finely
chopped fresh vegetables. Well, this one is no different, just the added goodness of fruits
makes it healthier and yummier. Serve it as an accompaniment to any of the mains
or have it by itself – this salad is sure going to be your favourite.

INGREDIENTS

2 medium apples, cored
and sliced thinly

2 medium oranges

12-15 seedless green
grapes, halved

12-15 seedless black
grapes, halved

1 medium green capsicum,
cut into strips

1 tablespoons lemon juice

1 medium cucumber,
sliced thinly

2 medium tomatoes, seeded
and cut into strips

2 spring onions, sliced thinly

Dressing

1 tablespoon chopped fresh
coriander

8-10 fresh mint leaves,
roughly torn

2 green chillies, chopped

1½ teaspoons Chaat Masala
(page 156)

Salt to taste

1 tablespoons lemon juice

METHOD

- Sprinkle one tablespoon
  of lemon juice over the
  apple slices to prevent
  discolouration.

- Peel the oranges and
  separate the segments.
  Remove the seeds and
  cut each segment in half.

- For the dressing, mix
  together the chopped
  coriander, mint leaves,
  green chillies, chaat
  masala, salt and
  lemon juice.

- Toss the fruit and
  vegetables in the
  dressing and serve
  chilled.

16 Carrot, Raisin And Black Olive Salad

Low in calories but high in carbohydrates...have a bowlful
of this salad when you need perk-me-up food.

INGREDIENTS

4-5 large carrots

½ cup raisins

6-8 black olives, sliced

2 tablespoons lemon juice

5-6 black peppercorns, crushed

1 green chilli, finely chopped

1 tablespoon honey

Salt to taste

¼ teaspoon black salt

6 walnut kernels, crushed

1 teaspoon extra virgin olive oil

6- 8 fresh mint leaves

METHOD

- Thickly grate carrots. Refrigerate till required for use.

- Combine lemon juice, crushed peppercorns, green chilli, honey, salt, black salt, walnuts, raisins, black olives and olive oil to make a dressing.

- Just before serving add the dressing to the grated carrots and toss.

- Serve garnished with mint leaves.

17 Murgh Aur Shimla Mirch Salad

Grilled chicken in a tangy dressing with crisp capsicums: you could, well, make a meal of this high protein salad! Looks good and tastes delicious!

INGREDIENTS

2 boneless chicken breasts

1 medium red capsicum, seeded and cut into strips

1 medium green capsicum, seeded and cut into strips

1 medium yellow capsicum, seeded and cut into strips

5-6 green olives

5-6 black olives

Marinade

1 tablespoon olive oil

3 tablespoons yogurt

½ tablespoon Green Chilli Paste (page 157)

1 teaspoon Ginger-Garlic Paste (page 157)

½ teaspoon Garam Masala Powder (page 156)

5-6 black peppercorns, crushed

Salt to taste

Dressing

4 teaspoons extra virgin olive oil

2 teaspoons lemon juice

2 teaspoons Chaat Masala (page 156)

Black salt to taste

METHOD

- Mix all the ingredients for marinade in a bowl. Add chicken breasts and marinate, preferably in the refrigerator, for an hour.

- Mix all the ingredients for the dressing and set aside.

- Grill the chicken breasts in a pre-heated grill, or on a non-stick tawa (griddle) on medium heat, for eight to ten minutes or until done, turning once or twice, taking care they remain juicy.

- Allow to cool and cut into one-inch pieces. Add the capsicums, olives and the dressing.

- Toss lightly and serve immediately.

18 Green Chana Chaat

Though best made with fresh green chana in season, this recipe uses dried ones.
Perk them up with spring onion greens and chopped paneer or tofu. Colour and taste
will definitely attract children since these two factors increase the palatability of the dish.

INGREDIENTS

1½ cups dried green Bengal gram, soaked overnight

2 medium onions, chopped

2 medium tomatoes, chopped

2-3 green chillies, chopped

2 tablespoons chopped fresh coriander

Black salt to taste

1 teaspoon Roasted Cumin Powder (page 158)

1 teaspoon Chaat Masala (page 156)

½ teaspoon red chilli powder

2 tablespoons lemon juice

METHOD

- Drain and pressure-cook the soaked green Bengal gram in three cups of water till pressure is released two to three times (two to three whistles) or till done.

- Transfer them into a non-stick kadai and simmer till all the water evaporates.

- Transfer the hot gram in a bowl.

- Add the onions, tomatoes, green chillies, chopped coriander, black salt, roasted cumin powder, chaat masala, chilli powder and lemon juice and mix well.

- Serve immediately.

Note: When in season use fresh green Bengal gram (hara cholia) instead of the dried ones.

19 Fresh Fruit Chaat

An excellent snack that can be enjoyed in between meals – healthy, pretty and tasty as ever. So much better than any of the junk food a lot of us crave for. This one really makes for a great choice!

INGREDIENTS

2 kiwi fruit, cut into
1-inch cubes

½ cup pomegranate kernels

½ cup orange segments

½ cup sweet lime segments

1 medium apple, cut into
1-inch cubes

¼ cup halved green grapes

¼ cup halved black grapes

½ teaspoon red chilli powder

1½ tablespoons Chaat
Masala (page 156)

Rock salt to taste

1 tablespoon lemon juice

METHOD

• Place the kiwi, pomegranate kernels, orange, sweet lime, apple, green and black grapes in a large bowl and place in the refrigerator to chill thoroughly.

• Just before serving sprinkle the chilli powder, chaat masala and rock salt.

• Add the lemon juice and toss well.

• Serve immediately.

Chapter 2
Snacks and Starters

20 Corn Uttapam

Move over regular onion-tomato uttapam because the newer version is taking over!
Add some boiled corn and capsicum to toppings and add a fantastic tasty dimension.

INGREDIENTS

2 cups readymade dosa batter

Salt to taste

1½ cups corn kernels, boiled

1 medium onion, chopped

1 medium tomato, chopped

1 medium green capsicum, seeded and chopped

1 tablespoon chopped fresh coriander

Chaat Masala (page 156) to taste

8 tablespoons oil

METHOD

- Take the dosa batter in a deep bowl. Add a little salt and water to get the required consistency.

- Combine the corn kernels, onion, tomato, capsicum, chopped coriander and chaat masala in another bowl.

- Heat a non-stick tawa. Pour a ladleful of the batter on it and spread it into a thick round of three-inch diameter.

- Top it with a portion of the corn mixture and drizzle half a tablespoon oil around the uttapam.

- Cook for three to four minutes or till the underside turns golden brown.

- Flip it over, drizzle half a tablespoon more oil around the uttapam and cook till both sides are equally done. Serve hot.

21 Palak Pakore Ki Chaat

A crunchy munchy treat that looks very good on a party table too! The idea of serving crisp batter-fried spinach leaves with dahi and chutneys is always well accepted.

INGREDIENTS

8-10 medium-sized fresh spinach leaves

1 cup coarse gram flour

Salt to taste

½ teaspoon red chilli powder

¼ teaspoon turmeric powder

½ teaspoon carom seeds

A pinch asafoetida

Oil for deep-frying

2 cups yogurt

2 teaspoons Roasted Cumin Powder (page 158)

4 tablespoons Green Chutney (page 157)

4 tablespoons Sweet Date and Tamarind Chutney (page 158)

2 medium onions, chopped

4 tablespoons nylon sev

4 tablespoons chopped fresh coriander

METHOD

- Take coarse gram flour in a bowl. Add salt, chilli powder, turmeric powder, carom seeds and asafoetida. Add sufficient water to make a thin batter.

- Heat sufficient oil in a kadai. Coat each spinach leaf with batter on both sides and deep-fry in hot oil till golden brown and crisp. Drain on absorbent paper.

- Whisk yogurt with salt to taste. Set aside.

- To serve, place two pakoras on a serving plate. Cover with half cup of whisked yogurt. Sprinkle cumin powder.

- Add one tablespoon each green chutney and sweet date and tamarind chutney.

- Sprinkle some chopped onions and cover liberally with sev.

- Garnish with chopped coriander and serve immediately. Similarly make other servings.

22 Vegetable Bhakarwadi

Bhakarwadis are traditionally quite crisp and dry and have a long shelf life. These are special as they are made using fresh vegetables and coconut. So yummy that they will get over while still warm!

INGREDIENTS

1 cup refined flour

1 tablespoon semolina

2 tablespoons oil + for deep-frying

Salt to taste

1/4 teaspoon black pepper powder

100 grams green peas

100 grams French beans, chopped roughly

3 potatoes, boiled and mashed

1/2 cup chopped fresh coriander

1/2 cup grated coconut

2 teaspoons Ginger-Green Chilli Paste (page 157)

1 teaspoon Garam Masala Powder (page 156)

METHOD

- Knead the refined flour with semolina, two tablespoons oil, salt, pepper powder and sufficient water to a semi soft dough. Cover with a damp cloth and set aside.

- Boil the green peas and French beans separately till soft. Drain thoroughly and mash.

- Mix together the green peas, French beans, potatoes, chopped coriander, coconut, ginger-green chilli paste, garam masala powder and salt.

- Divide the dough into four equal portions and roll out into thin chapatis.

- Spread the vegetable mixture evenly on all four chapatis. Roll them tightly into cylinders and cut the cylinders into half inch slices.

- Heat sufficient oil in a kadai and deep-fry the bhakarwadis, on medium heat, till golden and crisp.

- Drain on absorbent paper and serve.

Note: These last only for one day since fresh vegetables have been used. In case the filling mixture is thin, add a little poha and mix.

23 Spinach And **Cheese Idlis**

Bring about a revolution by introducing this fusion food to your children's diet!
Offer as an after-school or after-play snack! Excellent idea for the lunch box too...
as spinach provides iron and the cheese, essential calcium.

INGREDIENTS

8-10 spinach leaves

¼ cup grated cheese

½ cup skinless split black gram

1 cup idli rawa

Salt to taste

Oil for greasing moulds

½ teaspoon crushed black peppercorns

METHOD

- Soak the split black gram and idli rawa separately for three to four hours.

- Drain and grind the split black gram, sprinkling water as required, to make a smooth, spongy batter.

- Drain the idli rawa and add it with the salt to the batter and mix thoroughly with your hands, using a whipping motion so that the batter is mixed well.

- Place the batter in a large pan or bowl, cover tightly and rest in a warm place for twenty-four hours, or at least overnight.

- Blanch the spinach leaves in boiling water for two to three minutes. Reserve a few leaves and purée the rest. Shred the reserved leaves.

- Add the spinach purée to the idli batter and mix well.

- Pour into greased idli moulds, top with the shredded spinach leaves and grated cheese.

- Sprinkle crushed peppercorns and steam till the idlis are done.

- Serve the idlis with chilli sauce or chilli garlic sauce.

24 Cabbage Cauliflower Dhokla

The demand for a hatke snack is always there! How about using regular dhokla and tempering it with vegetables? Add some more nutrition and crunch and 'wow' factor to teatime!

INGREDIENTS

250 grams readymade dhokla

1 small cabbage, finely shredded

1 small cauliflower, grated

4-5 dried red chillies

3 tablespoons oil

¼ teaspoon asafoetida

1 teaspoon mustard seeds

1 tablespoon skinless split black gram

½ teaspoon carom seeds

6-8 curry leaves

½ teaspoon turmeric powder

Salt to taste

1 tablespoon lemon juice

METHOD

- Cut the dried red chillies into four pieces each and remove the seeds. Set aside.

- Heat the oil in a non-stick pan. Add the asafoetida, mustard seeds, black gram, carom seeds, curry leaves and red chillies to the pan and sauté till fragrant. Add the cauliflower and cabbage and mix. Add the turmeric powder and salt, mix well, cover and cook for five to seven minutes.

- Crush the dhokla and add to the pan and toss well. Add the lemon juice and mix again. Serve hot.

25 Corn N Sooji Balls

Corn is versatile and it helps to make some great deep-fried snacks that kids and adults both simply love! Try these delightfully different crunchy balls with any sauce or chutney of your choice – don't be surprised if they are appreciated and polished off just as much plain too!

INGREDIENTS

¼ cup sweet corn kernels, boiled

¼ cup semolina

½ cup milk

½ cup crumbled cottage cheese

2 tablespoons chopped fresh coriander

Salt to taste

¼ teaspoon Garam Masala Powder (page 156)

½ teaspoon Chaat Masala (page 156)

2 teaspoons lemon juice

¼ cup refined flour, mixed with ¼ cup water

½ cup breadcrumbs

Oil for deep-frying

METHOD

- Dry-roast the semolina in a non-stick kadai till fragrant. Add the milk and stir briskly and cook till dry. Set aside to cool.

- Add the corn, cottage cheese, chopped coriander, salt, garam masala powder, chaat masala and lemon juice and mix well. Divide into eight equal portions and shape into balls.

- Heat sufficient oil in a deep kadai.

- Dip the balls, one by one, in the flour mixture and roll each in breadcrumbs so that it is evenly and thickly coated.

- Gently slide the balls into the hot oil, a few at a time, and deep-fry till golden brown and crisp. Drain on absorbent paper.

- Serve with tomato ketchup.

26 Chilgoza Paneer

You must be knowing about how cashew nuts lend good flavour to paneer, so now how about trying it with a different nut like pine nuts? These nuts have a characteristic rich and deep flavour that says a yummy story with every crunch and bite!

INGREDIENTS

200 grams pine nuts

400 grams cottage cheese

Chaat Masala (page 156), as required

Black pepper powder, as required

Spicy pickle masala, as required

A few salty biscuits

A few fresh parsley leaves

METHOD

- Cut the cottage cheese into half-inch thick round slices and then into small rounds with a cookie cutter.

- Prick pine nuts attractively on the top side of the rounds.

- Sprinkle chaat masala and pepper powder.

- Spread a thin layer of pickle masala on salty biscuits and place a paneer round on each of them.

- Place a small parsley leaf on top and serve immediately.

27 Garlicky **Mushroom** Pakore

For those rainy, home-bound weekends, pakore made with mushrooms will be a fantastic surprise!
This new snack will thrill your family and the burst of flavour in this garlicky
preparation will definitely make them ask for an encore!

INGREDIENTS

1½ tablespoons Garlic
Paste (page 156)

16-20 fresh button
mushrooms

1½ cups gram flour

¼ teaspoon carom seeds

1 teaspoon red chilli powder

A pinch of soda bicarbonate

Salt to taste

1 lemon

Oil for deep-frying

METHOD

- Trim the stems of the
  mushrooms and place
  them in a bowl.

- To make the batter,
  combine the gram
  flour, carom seeds,
  chilli powder, soda
  bicarbonate, salt, garlic
  paste and sufficient water
  in a bowl and whisk till
  smooth.

- The consistency of the
  batter must be thick

enough to coat the
mushrooms. Add freshly
squeezed juice of lemon
and mix well.

- Heat sufficient oil in a
  deep kadai.

- Dip each mushroom into
  the batter and slide into
  the hot oil. Deep-fry on
  high heat till golden and
  crisp. Drain on absorbent
  paper. Serve hot.

28 Ragda Pattice

One of the hot-selling foods on the streets of Mumbai: 'pattice' for the small potato tikkis dunked in the 'ragda' - a white pea sauce garnished with chutneys and chopped onions – it's yummy and filling and had in many Gujarati homes as a meal by itself.

INGREDIENTS

1¼ cups dried white peas

4 large potatoes, boiled and mashed

¼ teaspoon turmeric powder

A pinch of asafoetida

Salt to taste

2 tablespoons cornflour

2-3 green chillies, chopped

Oil for shallow-frying

Green Chutney (page 157), as required

Sweet Date and Tamarind Chutney (page 158), as required

2 medium onions, chopped

2 teaspoons Chaat Masala (page 156)

2 tablespoons nylon sev

2 tablespoons chopped fresh coriander

METHOD

- Soak the dried peas in three cups of water for about six hours.

- Drain and boil in three to four cups of water with turmeric powder, asafoetida and salt till soft. Mash the peas slightly.

- Add a little water if too thick and simmer for ten minutes. Keep the ragda hot.

- Add the cornflour, green chillies and salt to potatoes and mix well.

- Divide into eight equal portions and shape into balls. Flatten slightly.

- Heat a little oil in a non-stick frying pan and shallow-fry the pattice gently on both sides on medium heat till evenly browned. Keep warm.

- To serve, place two pattice on a plate and pour a portion of the ragda on them.

- Drizzle a little green chutney and sweet date and tamarind chutney; sprinkle onions, chaat masala, sev and chopped coriander.

- Serve immediately.

29 Bhajanee Chakli

The crunchy chakli is another snack that has pan Indian attraction and for sure a Diwali special at home. You get them in varied tastes, depending on the combination of the ingredients that are used. Made with roasted urad dal and rice flour down south, whereas in Maharashtra the much popular bhajanee flour is used. Whatever the base be, chaklis are always enjoyable.

INGREDIENTS

Bhajanee Flour

4 cups rice

1 cup skinless split black gram

Dough

2 cups bhajanee flour

2 tablespoons butter

Salt to taste

1 teaspoon cumin powder

1 teaspoon red chilli powder

Oil for deep-frying

METHOD

- For the bhajanee flour, dry-roast the rice and black gram separately.

- Cool completely and grind separately to a powder. Sift both the flours and mix.

- Place two cups of bhajanee flour in a bowl. Add the butter, salt, cumin powder and chilli powder, and mix well.

- Divide the mixture in half. Take one half and knead into a soft dough with half a cup of water.

- When this dough is used up, knead the remaining mixture similarly.

- Place small portions of the mixture into a chakli mould and press out several chakli onto a plastic sheet.

- Heat sufficient oil in a kadai till moderately hot. Deep-fry the chakli till light golden brown and crisp.

- Drain on absorbent paper and set aside to cool. Store in an air-tight container.

Chef's Tip: Add 1 teaspoon of sesame seeds to the dough for special occasions.

30 Punjabi Samosa

This popular cone shaped snack is by far the most filling snack even by North Indian norms! Try sandwiching them between bread slices for a change. Or better still serve with chole as a most delicious chaat.

INGREDIENTS

Pastry

1 cup refined flour

½ teaspoon carom seeds (optional)

3 tablespoons ghee or oil

Salt to taste

Filling

4-5 medium potatoes, peeled and cut into ½-inch cubes

½ cup shelled green peas, boiled

2 tablespoons oil + for deep-frying

1 teaspoon cumin seeds

1 inch ginger, chopped

3-4 green chillies, chopped

1 teaspoon red chilli powder

1 teaspoon dried mango powder

1 teaspoon Garam Masala Powder (page 156)

Salt to taste

2 tablespoons chopped fresh coriander

METHOD

- For the pastry, mix refined flour, carom seeds, ghee and salt in a bowl. Add water a little by little and knead into stiff dough. Cover with a damp cloth and set aside to rest for ten to fifteen minutes.

- For the filling, heat two tablespoons of oil in a non-stick pan; add the cumin seeds and when they start to change colour, add the ginger, green chillies and potatoes. Stir well. Add the chilli powder, dried mango powder, garam masala powder and salt to taste. Stir well to mix.

- Sprinkle a little water over the mixture and cook, covered, till potatoes are done.

- Add the green peas and cook for five minutes on low heat. Add the chopped coriander and mix well. Take the pan off the heat and set aside to cool.

- Divide the cooled filling into sixteen portions.

- Divide the dough into eight equal portions and shape them into balls. Dust each ball with a little flour and roll out into a four-inch wide oval.

- Cut into half horizontally and moisten the edges with water. Shape each half into a cone and stuff it with the potato and pea filling. Press to seal the edges.

- Heat oil in a kadai, deep-fry the samose, a few at a time, in moderately hot oil till crisp and golden brown. Drain on absorbent paper.

- Serve hot with tamarind chutney.

31 Paani Puri

I hardly know of anyone who has a dislike for this quintessential street food of India. Be it the golgappa of North, the puchka of East or our very own paani puri on Mumbai streets – we Indians can pretty much swear by this snack at all times!

INGREDIENTS

40 crisp puffed puris

1½ cups Sweet Date and Tamarind Chutney (page 158)

Filling

1 cup green gram sprouts, boiled

2 large potatoes, boiled, peeled and cut into ¼-inch cubes

Black salt to taste

1 teaspoon Chaat Masala (page 156)

Paani

1 small bunch fresh coriander, chopped

1 small bunch fresh mint, chopped

5-6 green chillies

2 tablespoons Paani Puri Masala (see below)

½ tablespoon dried mango powder

Black salt to taste

Salt to taste

½ tablespoon Roasted Cumin Powder (page 158)

3 tablespoons lemon juice

¼ cup boondi

METHOD

- To make the filling, mix green gram sprouts, potatoes, black salt and chaat masala in a bowl.

- To make the paani, grind the chopped coriander, chopped mint and green chillies to a paste with a little water.

- Transfer the paste into a large bowl, add the paani puri masala, dried mango powder, black salt, salt, cumin powder and lemon juice and stir to mix well.

- Add six cups of water to the mixture. Stir to mix well and chill in the refrigerator.

- While serving add the boondi to the prepared paani and stir.

- Take a puri, break a little of the crust, fill it up with a little filling followed by a half a tablespoon of sweet date and tamarind chutney.

- Fill the puri with the prepared paani and serve immediately.

- Similarly prepare the remaining puris and serve.

Note: You can use 2-3 tablespoons of unripe mango paste instead of lemon juice for preparing the paani.

Paani Puri Masala

For pani puri masala, grind 2½ tablespoons dried mint powder, 3 tablespoons dried mango powder, 3 teaspoons salt, 6 teaspoons black salt, 1 tablespoon roasted cumin seeds, ½ teaspoon sugar and ½ teaspoon citric acid crystals to a fine powder. Use as required or store in an air-tight container.

32 Khandvi

This one's that delicious savoury Gujarati snack which is favoured not just by Gujaratis, but others too. Making khandvi is an art that takes some practice to get the correct consistency after cooking. So, trying out small portions first is highly recommendable.

INGREDIENTS

1¼ cups gram flour

1 inch ginger

2 green chillies

4 tablespoons oil

1 cup yogurt

Salt to taste

½ teaspoon turmeric powder

1 tablespoon lemon juice

1 teaspoon mustard seeds

A pinch of asafoetida

2 tablespoons grated coconut

2 tablespoons chopped fresh coriander

METHOD

- Sieve the gram flour and keep in a bowl. Grind the ginger and green chillies. Grease the reverse side of a few thalis or marble table top with a little oil.

- Mix the yogurt and half a cup of water to make buttermilk.

- Mix the gram flour with the ginger-green chilli paste, salt, turmeric powder, lemon juice and buttermilk, taking care that no lumps remain.

- Cook this mixture in a thick-bottomed non-stick pan, stirring continuously, till it becomes a smooth thick batter. It takes a little time to get ready.

- Quickly spread portions of the mixture over the greased inverted thalis or marble table top as thinly as possible while the batter is still hot.

- When cool, cut into strips two inches wide and roll them tightly.

- Heat two tablespoons of oil in a non-stick pan and add the mustard seeds. When they splutter, add the asafoetida and pour over the pieces.

- Serve, garnished with the coconut and chopped coriander.

33 Dal Pakwan

In Mumbai, one can see long queues outside shops selling this delicacy on Sunday mornings.
Sindhis love their masaledar dal with crisp pakwans for breakfast and especially on
Sundays they convert it into a combination for a brunch. Just make sure you
go for long run after this. You know why, don't you?

INGREDIENTS

Dal

1 cup split Bengal gram, soaked for 1 hour

½ teaspoon salt

¼ teaspoon turmeric powder

½ teaspoon red chilli powder

¼ teaspoon Garam Masala Powder (page 156)

¾ teaspoon dried mango powder

3 tablespoons oil

1 teaspoon cumin seeds

4-5 green chillies, slit

8-10 curry leaves

1 medium onion, chopped

½ cup chopped fresh coriander

Pakwan

1 cup refined flour

2 tablespoons whole-wheat flour

1 tablespoon semolina

¼ teaspoon cumin seeds

10-12 black peppercorns, crushed

Oil for deep-frying

Salt to taste

METHOD

- Bring to a boil three cups of water in a deep non-stick pan. Drain the gram and add to the boiling water. Add salt and turmeric powder. When the mixture comes to a boil again, reduce the heat to medium, cover and cook for twenty-five minutes. Add half cup of water and cook till soft.

- Add one-fourth teaspoon of chilli powder, half the garam masala powder and the dried mango powder. Check the salt and add more if needed. Cook the gram on low heat for ten minutes more.

- Heat the oil in a non-stick pan. Add the cumin seeds and when they change colour, add the chillies, curry leaves, remaining garam masala powder and the remaining chilli powder. Stir and pour over the cooked gram, mix well and take the pan off the heat and keep covered.

- To make the pakwan, sift the two flours into a large bowl. Add the semolina, cumin seeds, crushed peppercorns, two tablespoons hot oil and salt. Add four tablespoons of water and knead into medium-soft dough.

- Divide the dough into eight portions and roll each portion out into discs of four-inch diameter. Prick lightly with a fork.

- Heat sufficient oil in a kadai. Reduce the heat and add the pakwan, one by one, and deep-fry till golden and crisp on both sides. Press the pakwan down into the oil with a slotted spoon, while cooking, so that they become absolutely crisp. Drain on an absorbent paper.

- Garnish the dal with the onions and chopped coriander and serve with the pakwan.

34 Khasta **Kachori**

Spicy urad dal filling encrusted in crunchy covering makes for a perfect Indian
tea-time snack. Team these up with some tamarind chutney or gulp them up
with a basic tomato ketchup – these are lovely in all ways.

INGREDIENTS

2 cups refined flour

Salt to taste

½ teaspoon soda bicarbonate

5 tablespoons oil + for
deep-frying

Filling

½ cup skinless split
black gram, soaked

3 tablespoons ghee

1 inch ginger, finely chopped

1 green chilli, chopped

A pinch asafoetida

1 teaspoon coriander powder

½ teaspoon cumin powder

1 teaspoon red chilli powder

¼ teaspoon fennel powder

6-8 cashew nuts, roughly
chopped

1 tablespoon raisins

½ teaspoon sugar

Salt to taste

1 tablespoon lemon juice

METHOD

- Sift the flour, salt and
  soda bicarbonate together
  into a bowl. Add five
  tablespoons oil and
  mix well.

- Knead into soft dough
  using sufficient water.
  Cover with a moist cloth
  and set aside.

- Coarsely grind the soaked
  black gram using a little
  water.

- Heat ghee in a non-stick
  kadai and add the ground
  black gram, ginger,
  green chilli, asafoetida,
  coriander powder, cumin
  powder, chilli powder,
  fennel powder, cashew
  nuts and raisins.

- Cook till all the moisture
  has dried up. Add the
  sugar, salt and lemon
  juice.

- Mix well and remove the
  kadai off the heat, let the
  mixture cool. Divide into
  sixteen portions.

- Divide the flour dough
  into sixteen equal balls.
  Roll out each ball into a
  small puri such that it is
  thinner around the edges
  and thicker in the centre.

- Place a portion of stuffing
  in the centre and bring
  the edges together to
  form a ball.

- Heat sufficient oil in a
  kadai and deep-fry the
  kachori, a few at a time,
  on low heat for three
  to five minutes or until
  golden and crisp. Drain
  on absorbent paper.

- Serve with tamarind
  chutney.

35 Keema Potli Samosa

Stuffed savouries like samosas are popular and much appreciated for their unique styling of pastry. We go one step further and package mutton mince in a pastry that will look as if you are serving little money bags...not only a fun factor but also a chance to enjoy crisp pastry with a yummy filling. This has a high recall value and in some homes I see people using little bits of spring onion greens and actually putting ties on the potlis...making them look more realistic.

INGREDIENTS

1 cup refined flour

2 tablespoons semolina

5 teaspoons oil + for deep-frying

Salt to taste

Stuffing

300 grams mutton mince

2 tablespoons oil

1 teaspoon cumin seeds

2 inch ginger, chopped

3 green chillies, chopped

1 teaspoon red chilli powder

1 tablespoon coriander powder

1 teaspoon Roasted Cumin Powder (page 158)

Salt to taste

¾ cup yogurt

1 teaspoon Garam Masala Powder (page 156)

2 tablespoons chopped fresh coriander

METHOD

- To make the dough place the refined flour in a bowl. Add the semolina, five teaspoons oil and salt and mix. Add one-fourth cup of water, little by little, and knead into a stiff dough. Cover with a damp cloth and set aside to rest for ten to fifteen minutes.

- To make the stuffing, heat two tablespoons oil in a non-stick pan. Add the cumin seeds. When they begin to change colour, add the mutton mince and sauté for fifteen minutes or till half cooked.

- Add the ginger, green chillies, chilli powder, coriander powder, cumin powder and salt and mix well. Reduce heat to low, cover with a lid and cook for fifteen minutes.

- Add yogurt and stir. Increase heat to high and cook for ten minutes, stirring continuously. Reduce heat to medium and cook for twenty minutes or till the mutton is fully cooked and completely dry.

- Sprinkle the garam masala powder and chopped coriander and mix well. Allow it to cool completely. Divide into twenty portions.

- Divide the dough into twenty portions and shape them into balls. Roll out each ball into a disc of three-inch diameter. Place a portion of the ground mutton in the centre. Apply a little water on the areas a little away from the edges closer to the filling, collect the edges together in neat pleats and pinch the dough just above the filling to seal. Let the edges remain loose to give it a shape of a money bag (potli).

- Heat sufficient oil in a kadai. Gently slide in the potlis, a few at a time and deep-fry on medium heat till golden and evenly done. Drain on absorbent paper.

- Serve with Mint Chutney (page 157).

36 Pepper Rawas Tikka

I suggest you do not worry about the quantity of pepper...
meaty rawas can take this strong spice head on!

INGREDIENTS

500 grams Indian salmon
(rawas) fillets, cut into
1½-inch pieces

Oil for basting

Marinade

2 tablespoons crushed black
peppercorns

¼ cup Drained (Hung)
Yogurt (see below)

½ cup fresh cream

1 teaspoon Garlic Paste
(page 156)

1 teaspoon Ginger Paste
(page 157)

1 teaspoon carom seeds

1 tablespoon roasted
gram flour

A pinch of Garam
Masala Powder
(page 156)

2 tablespoons lemon juice

Salt to taste

1 tablespoon chopped
fresh coriander

METHOD

- To make the marinade, place the crushed peppercorns, drained yogurt, cream, garlic paste, ginger paste, carom seeds, roasted gram flour, garam masala powder, lemon juice and salt in a bowl and mix well.

- Add the chopped coriander and mix again.

- Rub this mixture into the fish pieces and marinate for forty-five minutes, preferably in the refrigerator.

- Preheat the oven to 220ºC/425ºF/Gas Mark 7.

- Thread the pieces of fish, half-an-inch apart, onto greased skewers.

- Roast in the preheated oven for six minutes.

- Lower the heat to 180ºC/350ºF/Gas Mark 4. Baste with oil and roast again for eight to ten minutes.

- Alternatively, cook the fish on a grill pan for seven to eight minutes on medium heat using oil as required.

- Serve hot on a bed of salad.

Drained (Hung) Yogurt: To drain the yogurt, hang it in a piece of muslin, preferably in a refrigerator, till all the whey is drained away. You can use the whey in some other dish.

37 Boti Kabab

From the kitchens of the Awadh, this traditional mutton starter has been a favourite since times immemorial. Succulent mutton cubes marinated in a mélange of spices and grilled to perfection – you have to try it to get the heavenly feeling!

INGREDIENTS

½ kg boneless mutton, cut into 1-inch cubes

2 tablespoons Unripe Papaya Paste (page 158)

1 tablespoon Ginger Paste (page 157)

1 tablespoon Garlic Paste (page 156)

½ teaspoon Green Chilli Paste (page 157)

½ teaspoon red chilli powder

¼ teaspoon Garam Masala Powder (page 156)

Salt to taste

¼ cup melted butter

Onion rings, for serving

Mint Chutney (page 157), for serving

METHOD

- Mix together the papaya, ginger, garlic and green chilli pastes with chilli powder, garam masala powder, and salt and apply this on the mutton cubes.

- Place them into a bowl and marinate in the refrigerator for three to four hours.

- Pressure-cook the marinated mutton cubes with one cup of water till the pressure is released four times (4 whistles) or till half done.

- Remove the lid when the pressure reduces and check if there is any liquid remaining. If yes, then cook till all the water evaporates. Remove from the pressure cooker and set aside.

- Heat a grill and grill the mutton cubes till completely cooked.

- Baste with melted butter from time to time so that mutton does not dry out.

- Once done, transfer onto a plate and serve with the onion rings and the mint chutney.

38 Prawn Pakoda

Call them pakoda or bhajiya or bhaja – wherever you travel in India, you will find people hooked onto these crunchy munchies. The most common ones are made with onion, potato and other veggies, while here, we give you an exciting variation with prawns. Try this out for you surely will love this non-vegetarian version!

INGREDIENTS

210 grams shrimps, shelled

½ teaspoon turmeric powder

2 teaspoons lemon juice

Salt to taste

1 teaspoon red chilli powder

½ teaspoon carom seeds

1 tablespoon chopped fresh coriander

1 tablespoon Ginger-Garlic Paste (page 157)

2 tablespoons gram flour

Oil for deep-frying

METHOD

- Place the shrimps, turmeric powder, lemon juice, salt, chilli powder, carom seeds, chopped coriander, ginger-garlic paste and gram flour in a bowl and mix well.

- Heat sufficient oil in a kadai.

- With moistened fingers shape the mixture into small pakode and drop into hot oil and deep-fry till golden and crisp.

- Drain on an absorbent paper. Serve hot.

39 Chettinad Fried Chicken

The Chettiar community of Tamil Nadu has one of the most aromatic and spiciest cuisines in all of India. And this one is no different. Chicken marinated in a spicy and flavourful paste that uses a liberal amount of curry leaves, and fried to perfection. This is how it is – simple yet awesome!

INGREDIENTS

1 whole (800 grams) chicken

2 medium onions, roughly chopped

1 inch ginger, roughly chopped

4-6 garlic cloves, roughly chopped

4 green chillies, roughly chopped

4-6 dried red chillies

½ teaspoon turmeric powder

1 tablespoon lemon juice

2 tablespoons rice flour

Salt to taste

10-12 curry leaves, finely shredded

Oil for shallow-frying

METHOD

- Split the chicken through the backbone and the breast, into two equal halves.

- Make three or four half-inch deep cuts on the breast and leg pieces.

- Grind the onions, ginger, garlic, green chillies and red chillies with a little water to a smooth paste.

- Mix the turmeric powder, lemon juice, rice flour and salt into the masala paste.

- Coat the chicken liberally with the paste and leave to marinate for two or three hours, preferably in a refrigerator.

- Mix the shredded curry leaves into the chicken.

- Heat the oil in a non-stick kadai; add the marinated chicken and sauté over high heat for two minutes on both sides to seal the juices.

- Lower heat to medium, cover and cook for fifteen to twenty minutes, turning over and basting frequently with the remaining marinade.

- Sprinkle a little water if the chicken starts drying out.

- Cook over high heat for the last few minutes, so that the surface of the chicken is crisp and golden brown.

- Cut into smaller pieces and serve hot.

40 Parsi Mutton Cutlets

Ground mutton patties that can be prepared one day in advance if you are planning a party!
You can make the patties in large batches and freeze them placing butter paper between the layers.
Before serving, all you need to do is thaw them, dip in the egg and cook! Some worry about
the mutton mince being raw? Not really, as it cooks just fine in the hot oil.

INGREDIENTS

500 grams mutton mince

5 slices bread

Salt to taste

½ tablespoon Ginger Paste
(page 157)

½ tablespoon Garlic Paste
(page 156)

6-8 green chillies, finely
chopped

1½ teaspoons red chilli
powder

1 teaspoon coriander powder

1 teaspoon Roasted Cumin
Powder (page 158)

¼ teaspoon turmeric powder

2 tablespoons chopped
fresh mint

2 tablespoons chopped
fresh coriander

1 cup breadcrumbs

Oil for deep-frying

4 eggs

Lemon wedges, as required

Onion rings, as required

METHOD

- Squeeze the mutton mince between the palms of your hands to remove excess water.

- Soak the bread in one cup of water for half a minute and squeeze to remove excess water.

- Place the mutton, bread, salt, ginger paste, garlic paste, green chillies, chilli powder, coriander powder, roasted cumin powder, turmeric powder, chopped fresh mint and chopped fresh coriander in a deep bowl.

- Mix well and set aside to marinate for three to four hours, preferably in a refrigerator.

- Divide the marinated mince into twelve equal portions, shape each portion into a ball and roll in breadcrumbs.

- Place each ball on a flat surface and flatten with your fingers into a four-inch patty, dusting with breadcrumbs as required. Place the cutlets in a refrigerator for half an hour.

- Heat sufficient oil in a kadai.

- Beat eggs lightly with salt and two tablespoons of water. Dip the cutlets in the egg and deep-fry for two to three minutes on each side. Drain on absorbent paper.

- Serve hot with lemon wedges and onion rings.

Chapter 3
Main Course Vegetarian

41 Chunky Masala Potatoes

Perfect substitute for French fries...remove boredom forever!

INGREDIENTS

6 large potatoes

2 tablespoons oil

Sea salt to taste

½ teaspoon roasted cumin seeds

6-8 black peppercorns

1 teaspoon red chilli flakes

1 tablespoon lemon juice

METHOD

- Parboil the potatoes for two minutes in five cups of water. Drain, cool and cut into thick wedges.

- Preheat the oven to 200°C/400°F/Gas Mark 6.

- Grease a baking tray with half tablespoon oil.

- Place the sea salt, cumin seeds, peppercorns and chilli flakes in a mortar and crush coarsely with a pestle.

- Place the potato wedges in a deep bowl and sprinkle three-fourth of the crushed spices over them. Add the remaining oil and mix well.

- Spread these potatoes on the prepared tray evenly. Bake in the preheated oven for fifteen minutes or till done.

- Sprinkle the remaining crushed spices and serve hot drizzled with the lemon juice.

42 Tilwale **Palak** Aloo

Perk up everyday meals with this delicious combination of sesame, spinach and potatoes.

INGREDIENTS

1 tablespoon roasted sesame seeds

2 bunches (500 grams) fresh spinach leaves, roughly chopped

8-10 baby potatoes

2 tablespoons oil

1 teaspoon cumin seeds

¼ teaspoon asafoetida

4 green chillies

Salt to taste

½ teaspoon turmeric powder

2 teaspoons coriander powder

1 teaspoon cumin powder

2 tablespoons yogurt

METHOD

- Halve each baby potato without peeling.

- Heat the oil in a non-stick pan. Add cumin seeds and when they begin to change colour add the asafoetida, green chillies and potatoes. Stir and add salt.

- Mix, cover and cook on medium heat for two minutes.

- Add the turmeric powder and stir. Cover and cook. Add the spinach leaves and stir. Cover and cook till done.

- Add the coriander powder, cumin powder and yogurt. Take the pan off the heat and add the roasted sesame seeds. Mix well and serve hot.

43 Dum Paneer Mitti Handi

The fragrance of mint, rose, sweet spices will enamor you when you break
the seal open of this cottage cheese dish cooked so delectably. A must have on the party table!

INGREDIENTS

400 grams cottage cheese, cut into 1-inch cubes

2 tablespoons oil

2 bay leaves

2 green cardamoms

2 cloves

¾ inch cinnamon stick

1 teaspoon Ginger Paste (page 157)

1 teaspoon Garlic Paste (page 156)

¾ teaspoon Green Chilli Paste (page 157)

½ cup Browned Onion Paste (page 156)

¾ teaspoon cumin powder

1½ tablespoons coriander powder

6-8 black peppercorns, crushed

Salt to taste

¾ cup yogurt, whisked

½ cup fresh cream

A generous pinch of saffron

3 green cardamoms, crushed

¾ tablespoon Garam Masala Powder (page 156)

3 tablespoons chopped fresh coriander

1½ tablespoons chopped fresh mint leaves

A few rose petals

1½ teaspoons rose water

Whole-wheat flour dough to seal the pan

METHOD

- Preheat the oven to 180⁰C/350⁰F/Gas Mark 4.

- Heat oil in a non-stick pan; add bay leaf, green cardamoms, cloves and cinnamon and sauté till fragrant.

- Add ginger paste, garlic paste and green chilli paste and mix well.

- Add browned onion paste and mix. Stir in one cup of water and cook for two minutes.

- Add cumin powder, coriander powder, crushed peppercorns and salt and sauté for one minute. Add yogurt and mix well.

- Add cottage cheese to the gravy and cook over medium heat. Stir in the fresh cream and the saffron.

- Transfer the mixture into a clay pot (mitti ki handi). Gently stir in the crushed cardamoms, garam masala powder, coriander and mint leaves, rose petals and rose water.

- Cover with the lid and seal the edges with flour dough.

- Place the handi in the oven and cook for ten to fifteen minutes.

- Break open the seal and serve hot.

44 Doodhi Paneer Ka Sukha Salan

Giving doodhi to your kids is a challenge sometimes! So let's take one big leap forward to make it into a restaurant-style dish that is colourful to look at and absolutely yummy to eat...

INGREDIENTS

600 grams bottle gourd, cut into ¾-inch diamonds

200 grams cottage cheese, cut into ¾-inch diamonds

1 medium red capsicum, cut into ¾-inch diamonds

1 medium yellow capsicum, cut into ¾-inch diamonds

1 medium green capsicum, cut into ¾-inch diamonds

2 tablespoons grated dried coconut

1 tablespoon peanuts

1 teaspoon sesame seeds

1 lemon-sized ball tamarind

4 tablespoons oil + for deep-frying

1 medium onion, sliced

¼ teaspoon cumin seeds

¼ teaspoon fenugreek seeds

¼ teaspoon fennel seeds

¼ teaspoon onion seeds

¼ teaspoon mustard seeds

8 curry leaves

2 teaspoons Ginger-Garlic Paste (page 157)

4 green chillies, chopped

1 teaspoon coriander powder

½ teaspoon cumin powder

¼ teaspoon turmeric powder

½ teaspoon red chilli powder

Salt to taste

½ teaspoon Garam Masala Powder (page 156)

1 tablespoon chopped fresh coriander

METHOD

- Dry-roast coconut, peanuts and sesame seeds. Cool and grind to a fine paste. Soak tamarind for thirty minutes in warm water, squeeze and strain the pulp.

- Heat sufficient oil in a deep kadai; deep-fry the onion till golden brown. Drain on absorbent paper.

- Heat four tablespoons oil in a non-stick pan. Add the cumin seeds, fenugreek seeds, fennel seeds, onion seeds and mustard seeds.

- Once they begin to splutter add the curry leaves and ginger-garlic paste. Sauté till the raw flavours disappear. Add the green chillies and bottle gourd and sauté for four to five minutes. Add all capsicums and cook, covered for ten to fifteen minutes.

- Add the coriander powder, cumin powder, turmeric powder and chilli powder. Sauté for three to four minutes. Add the sautéed onions and salt.

- Sauté for three to four minutes. Add the peanut paste and stir till the oil separates. Add the tamarind pulp and mix. Add the cottage cheese and toss well to coat with the spices.

- Sprinkle garam masala powder and chopped coriander. Stir and take the pan off the heat.

- Serve hot with rotis.

45 Kachche **Kele** Ke Kofte

Unripe green bananas are not to be undermined as an ingredient in the kitchen.
For those who do not want to cook always with potato these kofte stuffed with nuts
and dried fruit are so exotic that a party table can be adorned with them!

INGREDIENTS

Kofte

4 medium unripe green
bananas

1 inch ginger, chopped

4 green chillies, chopped

2 tablespoons chopped
fresh coriander

½ teaspoon garam
masala powder

1 tablespoon lemon juice

4 tablespoons cornflour

Salt to taste

Oil for deep-frying

Stuffing

7-8 cashew nuts, roasted
and chopped

4 dried figs, chopped

6 raisins, lightly roasted

½ inch ginger, chopped

A few sprigs fresh mint
leaves, hand torn

½ teaspoon Chaat Masala
(page 156)

1 tablespoon lemon juice

Gravy

½ cup cashew nuts, soaked

¼ cup melon seeds, soaked

¼ cup oil

6 green cardamoms

2 black cardamoms

4 cloves

2 one-inch cinnamon sticks

2 medium onions, sliced

1 tablespoon Ginger-Garlic
Paste (page 157)

4 medium tomatoes, puréed

1 teaspoon red chilli powder

2 teaspoons coriander
powder

½ teaspoon turmeric powder

½ teaspoon Garam Masala
Powder (page 156)

To Serve

2 inches ginger, cut into
thin strips

2 tablespoons chopped fresh
coriander

2 teaspoons fresh cream

METHOD

• For kofte, boil bananas
  with skin until soft. Peel
  and mash the bananas
  till smooth.

• Add ginger, green chillies
  and chopped coriander
  and mix. Add garam
  masala powder, lemon
  juice, two tablespoons of
  cornflour and salt. Mix
  the mixture thoroughly.
  Divide the mixture into
  sixteen equal portions.
  Shape each portion into a
  ball and set aside.

• For stuffing, mix together
  cashew nuts, figs, raisins
  and ginger. Add hand
  torn mint leaves, chaat
  masala and lemon juice.
  Divide into sixteen equal
  portions.

• Stuff each portion of this
  mixture into each banana
  portion, roll them in the
  remaining cornflour and
  refrigerate for half an hour.

• Heat sufficient oil in a
  deep kadai and deep-fry

the kofte till light brown in colour. Drain on absorbent paper and set aside.

- For gravy, grind soaked cashew nuts and melon seeds to a fine paste with a little water. Set aside.

- Heat one-fourth cup of oil in a non-stick pan. Add green cardamoms, black cardamoms, cloves, cinnamon and stir-fry till the cardamoms change colour.

- Add onions and fry till golden brown. Add ginger-garlic paste and sauté for three to four minutes.

- Add tomato purée, chilli powder, coriander powder, turmeric powder and stir-fry till oil rises to the surface.

- Add the cashew nut-melon seed paste and cook until the gravy leaves the sides of the pan. Pour in two cups of water and simmer

for about ten minutes or till you get a gravy of coating consistency. Sprinkle garam masala and remove from heat.

- In a serving dish place the kofte and pour the gravy on top.

- Serve hot garnished with the ginger strips, chopped coriander and fresh cream.

46 **Arbi** Ke Patton Ki Sabzi

Popularly known as aluchi patal bhaji in Maharashtra, this dish uses the nutritious leaves of the humble colocasia in a creative way. The sabzi is a good way of benefiting from the vitamins and magnesium present in the green leaves. It is rich in fibre too. Best to choose small to medium-sized leaves with tender maroon coloured stems.

INGREDIENTS

15-20 colocasia leaves, shredded

3½ tablespoons split Bengal gram, soaked

Salt to taste

3 tablespoons Tamarind Pulp (page 158)

1½ tablespoons raw peanuts

3 tablespoons oil

A generous pinch of asafoetida

¼ teaspoon fenugreek seeds

½ teaspoon mustard seeds

8-10 curry leaves

10-12 garlic cloves, finely chopped

2 green chillies, finely chopped

¼ teaspoon turmeric powder

3 tablespoons gram flour

1¼ tablespoons grated jaggery

1¼ tablespoons grated coconut

METHOD

- Place the colocasia leaves, split Bengal gram, salt and two tablespoons tamarind pulp and two to three cups of water in a deep non-stick pan.

- Cover and cook for three to four minutes. Add raw peanuts, cover and cook till soft. Set aside.

- Heat the oil in another non-stick pan, add the asafoetida, fenugreek seeds, mustard seeds, curry leaves, garlic, green chillies and turmeric powder and sauté till fragrant.

- Add the gram flour and mix well. Sauté for two to three minutes.

- Add the colocasia-dal mixture alongwith the water. Stir and add another half cup of water.

- Mix and add remaining tamarind pulp. Stir and add jaggery.

- Mix again and cook on medium heat for five to ten minutes.

- Add the coconut. Mix well, adjust salt and cook for five more minutes. Serve hot.

47 Dahi Papad Ki Sabzi

Run out of vegetables? No fear, this sabzi solves the problem.

INGREDIENTS

1½ cups sour yogurt

3 Bikaneri moong papads

¾ tablespoon gram flour

½ teaspoon turmeric powder

¾ teaspoon red chilli powder

Salt to taste

2½ tablespoons pure ghee

1 teaspoon cumin seeds

1½ teaspoons coriander powder

½ teaspoon asafoetida

2 whole dried red chillies, broken

¾ cup boondi

1 tablespoon chopped fresh coriander

½ teaspoon Garam Masala Powder (page 156)

METHOD

- In a large bowl, combine yogurt, gram flour, turmeric powder, chilli powder and salt.

- Add two cups of water and blend it. Strain and set aside.

- Heat ghee in a non-stick kadai. Add cumin seeds. When it changes colour, add coriander powder. Sauté for one minute.

- Add asafoetida and dried red chillies. Sauté for half a minute. Add yogurt mixture. Adjust seasoning.

- Stir continuously till it comes to a boil. Reduce heat and let it simmer for two minutes.

- Heat a non-stick tawa and roast papads on both sides. Roughly break into two-inch pieces.

- Add papads and boondi into the simmering yogurt mixture. Boil for two to three minutes.

- Garnish with chopped coriander and garam masala powder. Serve hot.

48 Chutneywale Aloo

A chatpati aloo preparation that can be a fantastic party appetizer since it is quite a hit with varied palates.

INGREDIENTS

1 cup fresh coriander, roughly chopped

¼ cup fresh mint leaves, coarsely shredded

10-12 green chillies, roughly chopped

4-6 garlic cloves, roughly chopped

2 one-inch ginger, roughly chopped

4 teaspoons lemon juice

40 baby potatoes

Salt to taste

½ teaspoon turmeric powder

2 tablespoons oil

2 teaspoons cumin seeds

2 teaspoons coriander powder

1 teaspoon cumin powder

½ cup skimmed milk yogurt

1 teaspoon sesame seeds, toasted

METHOD

- Parboil potatoes with salt and one-fourth teaspoon of turmeric powder. Drain, cool and halve without peeling them. Set aside.

- For the chutney, grind the chopped coriander, mint leaves, green chillies, garlic and ginger along with salt and lemon juice to a fine paste.

- Heat the oil in a non-stick pan and add the cumin seeds; sauté till fragrant.

- Add halved potatoes, coriander powder, cumin powder, remaining turmeric powder and mix.

- Add half a cup of water, cover and cook on low heat till the potatoes are done.

- Add the chutney, half a cup of water and mix.

- Adjust salt and simmer for three to four minutes or till the gravy has thickened. Add yogurt and stir.

- Cook till it comes to a boil and take it off the heat.

- Sprinkle toasted sesame seeds and serve hot.

49 Guar Falli Aloo Ki Sabzi

A Gujarati hot favourite, cluster beans cooked with potatoes and a medley of masalas will definitely win many hearts. My heart was won over when I first tasted it at my in-law's place. Best served with hot puffed up phulkas.

INGREDIENTS

250 grams cluster beans, stringed and trimmed at both ends

2 medium potatoes, quartered

3 tablespoons oil

½ teaspoon mustard seeds

½ teaspoon cumin seeds

½ teaspoon carom seeds

A pinch of asafoetida

1 medium onion, chopped

½ teaspoon turmeric powder

¾ teaspoon red chilli powder

1 tablespoon coriander-cumin powder

Salt to taste

2 tablespoons grated jaggery

1 teaspoon dried mango powder

METHOD

- Break the cluster beans into two to three pieces each or alternatively, cut into one-inch pieces.

- Heat the oil in a deep non-stick kadai and add the mustard seeds.

- As they begin to splutter, add the cumin seeds, carom seeds and asafoetida.

- Add the onion and sauté till golden brown. Add the cluster beans and potatoes and stir well.

- Add three to four tablespoons of water and mix.

- Cover and cook on low heat, stirring occasionally, till cluster beans are half cooked.

- Add the turmeric powder, chilli powder, coriander-cumin powder and salt.

- Stir well and cook till done.

- Add the jaggery and dried mango powder and mix well.

- Cook till well blended. Serve hot with rotlis.

50 Dhaabe Ki Sabziyan

From the roadside eateries of Punjab, comes this wholesome
dish that just needs hot roti as an accompaniment.

INGREDIENTS

10-12 medium cauliflower
florets, blanched

2 medium potatoes, boiled,
peeled and cubed

½ cup shelled green
peas, blanched

4 tablespoons oil + for
deep-frying

½ teaspoon cumin seeds

5-6 garlic cloves, grated

2 medium onions, grated

2 medium tomatoes, grated

1½ teaspoons grated ginger

½ teaspoon turmeric powder

2 teaspoons coriander
powder

½ teaspoon Roasted
Cumin Powder
(page 158)

1½ teaspoon red
chilli powder

2 tablespoons chopped
fresh coriander

Salt to taste

1 teaspoon Garam Masala
Powder (page 156)

Dal Fry

1 cup split pigeon
peas, boiled

1 tablespoon butter

½ teaspoon cumin seeds

½ teaspoon red chilli
powder

5-6 garlic cloves, grated

Salt to taste

METHOD

- Heat sufficient oil in a
  kadai and deep-fry the
  blanched cauliflower
  florets and the potato
  cubes.

- Drain on absorbent paper.
  Set aside.

- Heat four tablespoons oil
  in a non-stick kadai; add
  the cumin seeds. When
  they begin to change
  colour, add the garlic and
  sauté till lightly coloured.

- Add the onions and
  continue to sauté. When
  the onions turn light

brown, add the tomatoes
and stir.

- Add the ginger, turmeric
  powder, coriander
  powder, cumin powder
  and chilli powder and
  sauté till the oil separates.
  Take the pan off the heat
  and set aside.

- To make the dal fry, heat
  the butter in another
  non-stick pan and add the
  cumin seeds.

- When they begin to
  change colour, add the
  chilli powder, garlic and
  half the prepared onion-
  tomato masala. Mix well.

- Add the boiled split
  pigeon peas and salt
  to taste. Bring to a
  boil. Simmer for two to
  three minutes. Add one
  tablespoon chopped
  coriander. Set aside.

- In the remaining onion-
  tomato gravy, add

the boiled peas, fried cauliflower and potatoes. Mix well.

- Cook on low heat for two to three minutes.

- Add the remaining chopped coriander.

- Sprinkle the garam masala powder.

- Transfer the dal in the serving bowl and top up with the vegetable mixture. Serve hot.

51 Jain **Paneer** Makhni

Cooking a makhni gravy without onions and garlic is no longer a secret,
as this recipe shows you, step by step, how to make it. Enjoying a restaurant
-style dish in the comfort of your home is going to be easy now!

INGREDIENTS

200 grams cottage cheese, cut into ½-inch cubes or triangles

3 tablespoons oil

2 green cardamoms

1 inch cinnamon stick

1 bay leaf

3 cloves

2 teaspoons coriander powder

1 teaspoon cumin powder

1½ teaspoons red chilli powder

1½ cups freshly made tomato purée

Salt to taste

2 tablespoons cashew nut paste

2 green chillies, slit

½ teaspoon dried fenugreek leaves

2 tablespoons butter

2 tablespoons honey

1 cup fresh cream

METHOD

• Heat oil in a non-stick pan. Add cardamoms, cinnamon, bay leaf and cloves and sauté till fragrant.

• Add coriander powder, cumin powder and chilli powder and sauté on low heat for half a minute.

• Add tomato purée and sauté for thirty seconds. Add salt and cashew nut paste and continue to sauté for one minute.

• Cover and cook till oil begins to leave the masala. Add green chillies and mix. Cook for two minutes.

• Roast the dried fenugreek leaves on a non-stick tawa till fragrant. Crush coarsely between your palms. Set aside.

• Strain the tomato gravy into a bowl pressing the mixture so that all the flavours are extracted.

• Pour this into another non-stick pan and bring it to a boil. Add butter. Lower heat, add honey and mix.

• Add cottage cheese, mix gently and continue to cook on low heat for one minute.

• Add fresh cream, stir till well blended.

• Sprinkle dried fenugreek leaves and mix gently. Take pan off the heat immediately.

• Serve hot with rotis or paranthas.

52 **Palak** Chhole

Chhole will be presented with a new colour, not to say, added nutrition of spinach!
This is a recipe that can become a hit at parties or other family get-togethers.

INGREDIENTS

1 bunch (350 grams) fresh spinach,
blanched and chopped

1¼ cups chickpeas,
soaked overnight

2 teaspoons tea leaves

12 pieces dried Indian gooseberry

3 green cardamoms

1 black cardamom

2 bay leaves

1 inch cinnamon stick

2 tablespoons ghee

¼ cup oil

1 tablespoon cumin seeds

1 tablespoon dried
fenugreek leaves

1½ inches ginger, chopped

15 garlic cloves, chopped

1 tablespoon Green Chilli Paste (page 157)

3 tablespoons Chhole Masala (page 87)

1 tablespoon coriander powder

¾ cup fresh tomato purée

Salt to taste

2 teaspoons dried
mango powder

1 teaspoon Garam Masala Powder (page 156)

¼ teaspoon red chilli flakes

METHOD

- Tie up tea leaves, Indian gooseberry, green cardamoms, black cardamom, bay leaves and cinnamon in a piece of muslin to make a potli.

- Drain the chickpeas and place in a pressure cooker and add the potli along with five cups of water.

- Cover the cooker with the lid and cook under pressure, on low heat, till pressure is released eight to ten times (eight to ten whistles).

- Open the lid when the pressure is released completely, discard the spice potli, strain the chickpeas and reserve the cooking stock.

- Heat the ghee and oil in a deep non-stick pan.

- Add the cumin seeds, dried fenugreek leaves, ginger and garlic and sauté for five minutes on medium heat.

- Add green chilli paste, chhole masala and coriander powder and sauté for five minutes.

- Add the spinach and tomato purée and cook, stirring, till the oil separates from the masala.

- Add salt, dried mango powder, chickpeas and the reserved cooking stock and mix well.

- Simmer for five minutes. Add garam masala powder, mix and cook for two minutes.

- Transfer into a serving bowl, garnish with red chilli flakes and serve hot.

Chole Masala

Place a small non-stick frying pan on medium heat and dry-roast 2 tablespoons cumin seeds, 3 tablespoons coriander seeds, 2 one-inch cinnamon, 8-10 cloves, 1 black cardamoms, ½ teaspoon carom seeds, 2½ teaspoons black peppercorns, 1 teaspoon dried fenugreek leaves, 3-5 Sichuan pepper (tirfal), 2 tablespoons dried pomegranate seeds, 8-10 bay leaves and 8-10 dried red chillies till fragrant. Transfer the mixture onto a plate and set aside to cool. When cooled transfer the mixture into a blender jar and blend with 1 teaspoon dried mango powder, ½ teaspoon dried ginger powder, 1 teaspoon salt and 2 teaspoons black salt. Cool and store in an air-tight container.

53 Mirchi Ka Salan

Chillies in India form the basis of food. They are the essence of the cuisine in all the regions. Some like it hot, some like it moderate and some like it mild. But in Hyderabad, where the spicy Andhra cuisine rules the roost, this chilli preparation is a must serve with the famous Hyderabadi Biryani, and is a dish that you just cannot forget once you have tasted it.

INGREDIENTS

18-20 large green chillies

2 tablespoons oil + for deep-frying

2 tablespoons sesame seeds

1 tablespoon coriander seeds

1 teaspoon cumin seeds

½ cup roasted peanuts

2 dried red chillies, broken

1 inch ginger, chopped

6-8 garlic cloves

1 teaspoon mustard seeds

8-10 curry leaves

1 medium onion, grated

1 teaspoon turmeric powder

2 tablespoons Tamarind Pulp (page 158)

Salt to taste

METHOD

- Wash, wipe and slit the green chillies lengthwise without cutting the chillies into two.

- Heat sufficient oil in a kadai and deep-fry in hot oil for one minute. Drain and place on absorbent paper and set aside.

- Dry-roast the sesame seeds, coriander seeds and cumin seeds.

- Cool and grind them to a paste along with the roasted peanuts, red chillies, ginger and garlic.

- Heat two tablespoons of oil in a non-stick pan, add the mustard seeds. Once they splutter add the curry leaves.

- Sauté for half a minute and add the onion. Sauté, stirring continuously, till the onion is light golden.

- Add the turmeric powder and mix well. Add the masala paste and cook for three minutes, stirring constantly.

- Stir in one and half cups of water and bring it to a boil. Reduce the heat and cook for ten minutes. Add the tamarind pulp (mixed in half a cup of water, if it is too thick).

- Add the fried green chillies and salt and cook on low heat for eight to ten minutes. Serve hot.

Note: In Hyderabad, Mirchi ka Salan is traditionally served as an accompaniment to biryanis. Some people like to add grated coconut to the masala paste, but I prefer Mirchi ka Salan without coconut. This gravy is referred to as Tili (Til - Sesame) aur Falli (Moongfalli – Peanuts) gravy.

54 Bharwan **Karele**

Bitter gourds are considered to be among the most nutritious gourds. This reptile-looking veggie can lower blood glucose levels. And I have learnt the knack of converting karela-haters into karela-lovers! This recipe helps 100 per cent! In fact, these bitter gourds are absolutely irresistible.

INGREDIENTS

4 medium bitter gourds

Salt to taste

1 tablespoon oil

1 medium onion, chopped

2 teaspoons Ginger Paste (page 157)

1 tablespoon Garlic Paste (page 156)

1 teaspoon coriander powder

½ teaspoon red chilli powder

1 teaspoon cumin powder

½ teaspoon turmeric powder

2 teaspoons Tamarind Pulp (page 158)

Stuffing

½ cup gram flour

1 medium onion, chopped

2 tablespoons chopped fresh coriander

Salt to taste

½ teaspoon red chilli powder

¼ teaspoon Garam Masala Powder (page 156)

1 teaspoon carom seeds

METHOD

- Scrape the bitter gourds; make a slit on one side and remove the seeds.

- Rub the salt over and inside the gourd and set aside for one hour. Wash under running water and set aside.

- To make the stuffing, dry-roast the gram flour in a non-stick pan over low heat till fragrant.

- Remove from the heat, transfer to a plate and set aside to cool.

- Add the onion, chopped fresh coriander, salt, chilli powder, garam masala powder and carom seeds and mix well.

- Stuff the masala mixture into each bitter gourd and set aside.

- Heat the oil in a non-stick kadai; add the onion and sauté till light golden brown.

- Add the ginger paste and garlic paste and sauté for two minutes.

- Add the coriander powder, chilli powder, cumin powder and turmeric powder and mix well. Sauté the masala till fragrant.

- Add the stuffed bitter gourds, half cup of water and salt.

- Cover and cook on high heat for three or four minutes.

- Lower the heat and cook for ten to twelve minutes, stirring gently at regular intervals.

- Add the tamarind pulp and mix well.

- Cover once again and cook for another ten to fifteen minutes or till the bitter gourds are cooked.

- Serve hot.

55 Soya Keema Matar

Hail to the healthy and delightfully delicious Soya Keema Matar.

INGREDIENTS

1 cup soya granules

1 cup shelled green peas

1½ cups skimmed milk

2 tablespoons oil

8 garlic cloves, finely chopped

2 medium onions, finely chopped

1 inch ginger, grated

2 green chillies, chopped

1 teaspoon coriander powder

1 teaspoon cumin powder

¾ teaspoon red chilli powder

4 tablespoons chopped fresh coriander

Salt to taste

1 teaspoon Garam Masala Powder (page 156)

1 tablespoon lemon juice

METHOD

• Soak the soya granules in milk for an hour.

• Heat the oil in a non-stick deep kadai and add the garlic and onions. Cook on medium heat till they turn translucent.

• Add the ginger, green chillies, coriander powder, cumin powder and chilli powder and two tablespoons of water. Cook for two minutes on medium heat.

• Add the green peas and three-fourth cup water and mix well. Cover and cook till peas are nearly done. Add the soya granules along with the milk and cook till almost dry.

• Add the chopped coriander, salt, garam masala powder and lemon juice and mix well. Serve hot.

Chapter 4
Main Course Non-Vegetarian

56 Kadai Murgh Methi Palak

Fully flavoured chicken tikka in an exciting rich green gravy made with fresh palak and methi. Nutritious and healthy dish to present at a family meal.

INGREDIENTS

Chicken Tikka

400 grams boneless chicken, cut into sixteen 1½-inch pieces

2 teaspoons Garlic Paste (page 156)

1 teaspoon Ginger Paste (page 157)

2 tablespoons Kashmiri red chilli paste

Salt to taste

½ tablespoon lemon juice

½ cup Drained (Hung) Yogurt (page 60)

1 teaspoon Garam Masala Powder (page 156)

2 tablespoons oil

1 teaspoon turmeric powder

1 teaspoon Kashmiri red chilli powder

1 tablespoon gram flour

Melted butter for basting

Gravy

2 medium onions

2 small bunches (500 grams) fresh spinach leaves, blanched

¼ cup oil

25 garlic cloves, chopped

1⅓ tablespoons Kadai Masala (page 95)

Salt to taste

½ cup fresh tomato purée

½ bunch (200 grams) fresh fenugreek leaves, blanched and chopped

½ teaspoon turmeric powder

2 teaspoons Kashmiri red chilli powder

2 teaspoons coriander powder

3 tablespoons butter

1 teaspoon crushed black peppercorns

2 teaspoons Chaat Masala (page 156)

2 teaspoons dried fenugreek leaves

2 tablespoons cashew nut paste

¼ cup yogurt

1 medium green capsicum, cut into 1-inch pieces

1 medium tomato, cut into 1-inch pieces

¼ cup fresh cream

2 tablespoons chopped fresh coriander

1 teaspoon lemon juice

1 teaspoon red chilli flakes

METHOD

- To make the chicken tikka, preheat oven to 200⁰C/400⁰F/Gas Mark 6.

- Mix together the garlic paste, ginger paste, red chilli paste, salt, lemon juice, hung yogurt, garam masala powder and apply to the chicken pieces.

- Heat two tablespoons oil in a small non-stick pan and take it off the heat. Add the turmeric powder, chilli powder and gram flour and mix well.

- Add this to the chicken and set aside to marinate for one hour. Place the chicken pieces on a

- baking tray and cook in the preheated oven for ten minutes.

- Baste with melted butter and cook for five minutes more. Set aside.

- For the gravy, finely chop one onion and chop the other into one-inch square pieces.

- Chop two-third of blanched spinach leaves and make a purée of the remaining spinach leaves.

- Heat one-fourth cup oil in a non-stick kadai; add the garlic and sauté till light brown.

- Add one tablespoon kadai masala, finely chopped onion and salt and sauté till lightly browned.

- Add the tomato purée and sauté till oil separates.

- Add the fenugreek leaves and chopped spinach leaves and sauté for two minutes more.

- Add the turmeric powder, chilli powder, coriander powder and butter and sauté for five minutes.

- Add the crushed peppercorns, chaat masala, dried fenugreek leaves, cashew nut paste, yogurt, spinach purée, onion pieces, capsicum and tomato and mix well.

- Add the chicken tikkas and cream and cook for two to three minutes.

- Transfer into a serving dish, sprinkle chopped coriander, remaining kadai masala, lemon juice and red chilli flakes and serve hot.

Kadai Masala

To make kadai masala, coarsely grind together 4 tablespoons coriander seeds, 20-25 black peppercorns, 7 green cardamoms, 2 dried red chillies, 1 black cardamom and 1 tablespoon cumin seeds. This makes 7 tablespoons of powder.

57 Nargisi **Kofta** Curry

Let's look at the word nargisi – it is a derivative of nargis which is the daffodil flower. Daffodils are beautiful with a sunshine yellow centre and spiked white petals...a colour combination that the boiled egg would reveal when cut in half! There is more that can be done with these mutton-coated boiled eggs...can place them in a biryani and create pockets that give a novel surprise!

INGREDIENTS

1 cup mutton mince

6 eggs

4 bread slices

1 teaspoon Ginger Paste (page 157)

1 teaspoon Garlic Paste (page 156)

6 green chillies, chopped

Salt to taste

3 teaspoons red chilli powder

2 teaspoons coriander powder

½ teaspoon Roasted Cumin Powder (page 158)

3 tablespoons chopped fresh coriander

2 tablespoons chopped fresh mint

½ cup breadcrumbs

2 tablespoons oil + for deep-frying

4 medium onions, chopped

4 medium tomatoes, chopped

1 teaspoon Garam Masala Powder (page 156)

½ teaspoon black pepper powder

METHOD

- Wash the muttom mince under running water and drain well in a colander.

Squeeze between your palms to remove excess water.

- Place a non-stick pan on high heat and pour in five cups water. When the water comes to a boil, add four eggs and cook for eight to ten minutes. Remove pan from heat, allow eggs to cool. Peel and set aside.

- Beat the remaining two eggs in a small bowl and set aside.

- Place the mince, bread, ginger paste, garlic paste, three green chillies and salt to taste in a blender jar and grind to a smooth paste.

- Transfer into a bowl and stir in one and a half teaspoons chilli powder, coriander powder, cumin powder, half of the chopped coriander and mint. Combine well and divide the mixture into four equal portions.

- Cover each egg with one portion of the mince till completely enclosed. Smoothen the surface with moistened hands. Spread the breadcrumbs in a plate.

- Heat sufficient oil in a kadai. Dip each mince-covered egg in beaten egg, roll in the breadcrumbs and slide into the hot oil and cook for eight minutes or till golden and crisp on the outside. Drain on absorbent paper. Cut each egg ball into half vertically. Place in a shallow serving dish.

- To make the tomato sauce, heat two tablespoons oil in a non-stick pan over medium heat. Add the onion and cook for five minutes or till the onion is lightly browned.

- Add the tomatoes, remaining chillies, remaining chopped coriander, garam masala powder, remaining chilli powder, salt and pepper powder. Add six cups water and simmer for fifteen minutes or till the sauce is cooked.

- Remove pan from heat, pour the tomato sauce over the stuffed eggs and serve hot.

58 Kairi **Murgh**

Chicken has a strong affinity for all types of masalas and souring agents. Here we use unripe green mango to give you a curry that is bursting with fresh flavour. Keep some hot rotis ready!

INGREDIENTS

1 kilogram chicken,
cut into 1½-inch pieces

2 medium unripe green
mangoes

1½ teaspoons Ginger paste
(page 157)

1½ teaspoons Garlic Paste
(page 156)

Salt to taste

2 teaspoons Garam Masala
Powder (page 156)

1½ teaspoons
Green Chilli Paste
(page 157)

4-5 cloves

5 tablespoons oil

2 medium onions, sliced

¼ teaspoon turmeric powder

1½ teaspoons red chilli
powder

2 teaspoons coriander
powder

2 tablespoons chopped fresh
coriander

A few pieces of charcoal

METHOD

- Peel and cut mangoes into small pieces. Purée half of the pieces.

- In a bowl, marinate chicken with half the ginger paste, half the garlic paste, salt, half the garam masala powder, half the green chilli paste, and puréed mango for about an hour, preferably in the refrigerator.

- Place a coal over the gas flame and when it is red-hot put it in a katori (small stainless steel bowl) and place in the centre of the marinated chicken.

- Place the cloves over the coal and pour one tablespoon of oil on it and immediately cover it with a lid. Let it stand for a few minutes.

- Heat the remaining oil in a non-stick kadai; add onions and sauté till translucent.

- Add the remaining ginger paste, garlic paste, green chilli paste and sauté for two minutes.

- Add marinated chicken, turmeric powder, chilli powder, coriander powder, remaining garam masala powder and mango pieces. Stir so that the masala coats all the chicken pieces evenly.

- Cook on high heat for five to six minutes. Adjust salt; add chopped coriander and three-fourth cup of water.

- Cover and cook for ten to twelve minutes or till done. Serve hot.

59 Coconut **Rawas**

A delightfully flavoured rawas recipe served with a fusion of coconut milk, honey and lemon grass...all lending their delicate nuances in the right proportions.

INGREDIENTS

1½ cups Coconut Milk (page 156)

2 Indian salmon fillets, cut into cubes

Salt to taste

1 tablespoon lemon juice

1 medium onion, chopped

1 inch ginger, chopped

3-4 garlic cloves, chopped

3 fresh red chillies, stemmed

1 stalk lemon grass, chopped

2 tablespoons oil

2 teaspoons honey

1 tablespoon chopped fresh coriander

METHOD

- Sprinkle salt and half a tablespoon of lemon juice on the fish pieces. Set aside to marinate for fifteen minutes.

- Grind onion, ginger, garlic, two fresh red chillies and lemon grass to a paste. Set aside.

- Diagonally slice the remaining fresh red chilli. Set aside for garnish.

- Heat oil in a non-stick pan and sauté fish pieces on medium heat for two minutes.

- Add the paste and stir. Continue to sauté till fish is cooked. Add coconut milk and cook for one minute. Add honey and chopped coriander and stir.

- Add the remaining lemon juice and mix. Serve hot, garnished with fresh red chilli.

60 Prawn Ghassi

The popular vegetarian version from Udupi cuisine in Karnataka gets a makeover with this non-vegetarian version. Succulent prawns cooked in a tangy spiced coconut gravy goes lovely with a neer dosa or an appam. Try it to know what I'm talking about!

INGREDIENTS

18-20 medium prawns, shelled and deveined

Salt to taste

3 tablespoons oil

4 roasted dried red chillies

2 teaspoons coriander seeds

1 teaspoon cumin seeds

8-10 black peppercorns

¼ teaspoon fenugreek seeds

1 cup grated coconut

2 medium onions, finely chopped

½ teaspoon turmeric powder

5 garlic cloves

1½ tablespoons Tamarind Pulp (page 158)

METHOD

- Wash the prawns thoroughly under running water. Drain and pat them dry.

- Sprinkle the salt and keep aside for one hour preferably in the refrigerator.

- Heat one tablespoon of oil in a non-stick pan and sauté the red chillies, coriander seeds, cumin seeds, peppercorns and fenugreek seeds till fragrant.

- Grind them with the coconut, half the onions, turmeric powder, garlic, tamarind pulp and sufficient water to a smooth paste.

- Heat the remaining oil in a deep non-stick pan and sauté the remaining onion till light brown.

- Add the ground masala paste and sauté for two to three minutes.

- Add two cups of water and mix well.

- When the mixture comes to a boil, add the prawns and adjust seasoning.

- Simmer for five minutes or till the prawns get cooked.

- Serve hot.

61 Goan **Fish** Curry

Fish and rice is a comforting combination for most fish lovers...especially if the fish is made using a Goan recipe, tart and tasty! The use of red rice adds more flavour in totality.

INGREDIENTS

2 medium (400 grams each) pomfret or any flat fish

2 tablespoons oil

1 small onion, chopped

2 green chillies, slit and halved

Salt to taste

1 tablespoon malt vinegar

Paste

2 teaspoons cumin seeds

2 tablespoons coriander seeds

6 dried red chillies

½ cup grated coconut

2 inches ginger, chopped

15 garlic cloves, chopped

2 tablespoons Tamarind Pulp (page 158)

METHOD

- Clean, wash and cut each fish into five to six pieces.

- Dry-roast cumin seeds, coriander seeds and dried red chillies.

- Make a fine paste of all the roasted spices along with coconut, ginger, garlic and tamarind pulp with a little water.

- Apply half of the ground paste to fish.

- Heat oil in a non-stick pan. Add onion and sauté till golden brown.

- Add green chillies and cook on medium heat for three minutes, stirring constantly.

- Add the remaining ground paste and stir well.

- Sauté for five minutes till fragrant. Add one and a half cups of water.

- Bring to a boil and then add the marinated fish and salt.

- Cook on low heat for about five minutes or till fish is just done.

- Stir in vinegar and serve hot with red rice.

62 Chana **Mutton**

Chickpeas goes well with potatoes and cottage cheese, but for those in the quest for something different try it out with meat cubes! This excellent preparation comes to you in a no-fuss recipe, fast to cook and good to eat!

INGREDIENTS

1 cup chickpeas, soaked

500 grams mutton, cut into 1-inch pieces on the bone

3 tablespoons oil

2 bay leaves

7-8 cloves

2 black cardamoms

5 green cardamoms

7-8 black peppercorns

3 medium onions, sliced

½ teaspoon turmeric powder

3-4 green chillies, slit

2 teaspoons coriander powder

1 teaspoon cumin powder

1½ teaspoons red chilli powder

Salt to taste

1½ cups yogurt, whisked

METHOD

- Heat the oil in a pressure cooker. Add the bay leaves, cloves, black cardamoms, green cardamoms, peppercorns, and onions and sauté till lightly coloured.

- Add the mutton and continue to sauté for three to four minutes. Add the turmeric powder, green chillies and continue to sauté for three to four minutes more. Drain the chickpeas and add to the pressure cooker.

- Add the coriander powder, cumin powder, chilli powder, salt and mix well. Add two cups of water and yogurt and mix well.

- Close the cooker with the lid and cook under pressure, on medium heat, until pressure is released six to eight times (six to eight whistles) or till both, the chickpeas and mutton, are completely cooked and tender.

- Open the lid of the cooker when the pressure reduces completely. Stir and serve hot with roti.

Chapter 5
Rice and Breads

63 Curd Rice

Also known as bakala bhaat in southern India, this dish definitely has a cooling effect on the body, besides being filling. But make sure to reduce the quantity of yogurt and increase the quantity ot milk if you are preparing it much in advance of serving. This will prevent the rice from becoming too sour.

INGREDIENTS

1½ cups Kolam rice, soaked

1 cup yogurt

½ cup milk

Salt to taste

2 tablespoons oil

1 teaspoon mustard seeds

¼ teaspoon asafoetida

1 dried red chilli, broken

8-10 curry leaves

1 inch ginger, chopped

4 green chillies, chopped

¼ cup fresh cream

1 medium cucumber, peeled, seeded and grated

1 medium carrot, grated

METHOD

- Drain and boil the rice in four and a half cups of water till it is slightly overcooked. Drain well and cool. When it reaches room temperature, add the milk and salt.

- Heat the oil in a small non-stick pan; add the mustard seeds, asafoetida, dried chilli and curry leaves. When the seeds begin to splutter, add the ginger and green chillies and sauté for half a minute.

- Add the seasoning to the rice. Add the yogurt and cream. Mix well and transfer into a bowl and chill in the refrigerator.

- Squeeze out excess water from the cucumber.

- Garnish the rice with the cucumber and carrot and serve chilled.

64 Jeera Rice

A great way to fancy up a simple steamed rice – the cumin flavour in this tossed rice matches brilliantly with the all-time favourite dal fry. Or just about a simple pickle and papad. This match is surely made in heaven!

INGREDIENTS

3 cups cooked Basmati rice

2 teaspoons cumin seeds

1½ tablespoons ghee

1 tablespoon Roasted Cumin Powder (page 158)

1 tablespoon coriander powder

Salt to taste

METHOD

- Heat the ghee in a non-stick pan, add the cumin seeds and sauté for one minute.

- Add the rice, cumin powder, coriander powder, salt and toss to mix. Cook for a minute.

- Serve hot.

65 Tamarind Rice

This classic South Indian dish is loved for its spicy and tangy flavour. The roasted peanuts add crunch to the dish. What's more, it stays for a few days so it can automatically become your favourite to carry while travelling long-distance!

INGREDIENTS

1½ cups rice, soaked

2 lemon-sized tamarind balls

4 tablespoons oil

½ cup raw peanuts

¼ cup white sesame seeds

1 teaspoon mustard seeds

2 dried red chillies

6-8 curry leaves

½ teaspoon turmeric powder

Salt to taste

Masala

2 tablespoons oil

2 tablespoons split Bengal gram

1 tablespoon skinless split black gram

1 teaspoon fenugreek seeds

10 dried red chillies

¼ teaspoon asafoetida

6-8 curry leaves

METHOD

- Drain and boil the rice in five cups of water in a deep non-stick pan till three-fourth done.

- Drain and mix in two tablespoons of oil and set aside to cool.

- Soak the tamarind in one cup of warm water and extract the pulp and set aside.

- Heat two tablespoons of oil in a small non-stick pan and sauté the masala ingredients. Cool and grind to a coarse powder. Set aside.

- Soak the peanuts for five minutes and drain.

- Dry-roast the sesame seeds on medium heat, cool and pound to a coarse powder. Set aside.

- Heat the remaining oil in a deep non-stick pan. Add the mustard seeds, red chillies and curry leaves. Once the mustard seeds splutter, add the peanuts and sauté till fragrant.

- Add the tamarind pulp and cook for a few minutes. Add the masala powder and turmeric powder and bring to a boil and continue simmering till the raw smell of the tamarind disappears.

- Add the salt and mix well. Stir frequently till the oil surfaces and the mixture reduces to a fairly thick consistency. Add the cooled rice and toss to mix well.

- Sprinkle the sesame powder and serve immediately.

Note: You can make this tamarind mixture in larger quantity and store in the refrigerator. Mix with hot rice whenever required. Use extra oil for longer shelf life. This item is traditionally prepared in a soft stone vessel to enhance the flavour.

66 Bisi Bele Hulianna

Literally translating to 'hot lentil rice' in Kannada language, this dish is an interesting one
as the consistency is that of a porridge! The special Hulianna masala in it makes it simply delectable.
You can even add vegetables of your choice to level-up the nutrient quotient!

INGREDIENTS

1½ cups rice, soaked

¾ cup split pigeon peas, soaked

1½ lemon-sized tamarind ball

5 tablespoons oil

1 medium onion, sliced

3-4 green chillies, slit

8-10 shallots, peeled

10-12 curry leaves

½ teaspoon turmeric powder

3 medium tomatoes, quartered

¼ teaspoon asafoetida

½ teaspoon red chilli powder

Salt to taste

½ teaspoon mustard seeds

2 dried red chillies, broken

4 tablespoons pure ghee

10-12 cashew nuts

Hulianna Masala

¼ cup split Bengal gram

2 tablespoons skinless split black gram

4 green cardamoms

4 cloves

1 inch cinnamon

1 teaspoon fenugreek seeds

1 teaspoon cumin seeds

4 dried red chillies

METHOD

- Soak the tamarind in one cup of warm water for half an hour, remove the pulp, strain and set aside.

- Dry-roast the hulianna masala ingredients individually on a non-stick tawa. Cool, mix and grind to a coarse powder.

- Heat three tablespoons of oil in a pressure cooker and sauté the onion till it is translucent.

- Add the green chillies, shallots and sauté for a minute. Add the curry leaves and turmeric powder. Add the soaked rice and split pigeon peas along with five cups of

water. Bring to a boil, stirring occasionally.

- Add the tomatoes, asafoetida, chilli powder and salt. Stir well and add the powdered hulianna masala.

- Cover and pressure-cook till the pressure is released three to four times (three to four whistles). Open the lid when the pressure reduces and stir well.

- Check the consistency. If it is too dry, moisten with a little warm water.

- Heat the remaining oil in a small non-stick pan and add the mustard seeds and red chillies. When the mustard seeds splutter add the seasoning to the rice mixture and stir.

- Heat the pure ghee in a non-stick pan and fry the cashew nuts till light brown and add to the rice along with the ghee.

- Mix well and serve hot.

67 Dal Khichdi

This is pure comfort food for most of us! And easy does it – just cook rice and dal together with some spices and a dash of amchur, top it up with heaps of freshly chopped coriander leaves and it's good to go. And don't forget to pair it up with its char yaar – ghee, papad, dahi, achar!

INGREDIENTS

1½ cups split pigeon peas, soaked

2 cups Basmati rice, cooked

1 teaspoon turmeric powder

Salt to taste

2 tablespoons ghee

2 teaspoons cumin seeds

15-20 garlic cloves, finely chopped

¼ teaspoon asafoetida

1 teaspoon red chilli powder

1 teaspoon dried mango powder

1 tablespoon chopped fresh coriander

METHOD

- Drain and boil the pigeon peas with four cups of water, turmeric powder and salt till soft.

- Heat the ghee in a non-stick pan, add the cumin seeds and sauté till light brown.

- Add the garlic and sauté till golden. Add the asafoetida and sauté.

- Add the boiled pigeon peas and enough water to get a pouring consistency and mix well.

- Add the chilli powder, salt and dried mango powder and mix well and simmer for two to three minutes.

- Add the cooked rice and mix well.

- Add the chopped coriander and mix well. Serve hot.

68 Pudina **Paneer** Pulao

Long grained rice in a pulao is always welcome at the table for any meal, but how about making it delicately flavoured with mint and luscious with soft paneer? Wouldn't that be a novelty?

INGREDIENTS

½ cup fresh mint leaves, roughly chopped

100 grams cottage cheese, cut into 1-inch cubes

1½ cups Basmati rice, soaked for ½ hour

2 green chillies, roughly chopped

1½ inches ginger, roughly chopped

¾ cup yogurt, whisked

3 tablespoons oil

2 bay leaves

4-6 green cardamoms

4-6 cloves

2-3 black cardamoms

8-10 black peppercorns

Salt to taste

METHOD

- Grind the mint leaves, green chillies, ginger and yogurt into a smooth chutney.

- Heat the oil in a thick-bottomed non-stick pan.

- Add the bay leaves, green cardamoms, cloves, black cardamoms and peppercorns.

- When they begin to emanate a nice aroma, add the mint chutney and cook for two to three minutes on low heat.

- Add three cups of water and bring to a boil. Stir in salt to taste.

- Add the drained rice and bring to a boil.

- Cover the pan and cook over low heat for about eight to ten minutes, or till rice is completely cooked.

- Gently stir in the cottage cheese cubes and serve hot.

69 Brown Rice Biryani With Chutney **Chicken**

Brown rice requires an acquired taste but once done, you will keep enjoying it in every rice preparation. Nuttiness of brown rice not only lends a deeper flavour to this biryani but also the goodness of fibre.

INGREDIENTS

2 cups brown rice, soaked for ½ hour in 4 cups of water

½ cup freshly made paste of coriander leaves

400 grams chicken, cut into 1½-inch pieces on the bone

Salt to taste

1 inch cinnamon stick

5 green cardamoms

6 cloves

½ cup skimmed milk yogurt

¼ teaspoon turmeric powder

1 teaspoon lemon juice

4 tablespoons oil

3 medium onions, sliced

2 teaspoons Ginger-Garlic Paste (157)

3 tablespoons chopped fresh coriander

5-6 saffron threads, soaked in 2 tablespoons skimmed milk

A few fresh rose petals

A few sprigs of fresh mint

¾ teaspoon screw pine essence

¾ teaspoon rose water

½ teaspoon Garam Masala Powder (page 156)

Whole-wheat flour dough, as required

METHOD

- Drain the brown rice. Place in a deep non-stick pan with little salt, eight cups of water, half-inch cinnamon, two green cardamoms and three cloves.

- Cook on medium heat till three-fourth done, adding more water only if required. Drain in a colander and set aside.

- Take a large deep bowl. Add coriander paste, yogurt, salt to taste, turmeric powder and lemon juice. Mix well and add chicken pieces in it and mix well. Cover the bowl and allow chicken to marinate for one hour, preferably in the refrigerator.

- Heat two tablespoons oil in a deep non-stick pan and sauté half of the onions on medium heat till well browned. Drain on absorbent paper and set aside.

- Add the remaining oil to the same pan, remaining cinnamon, three green cardamoms, three cloves and remaining onions, and sauté till the onions are lightly browned.

- Add ginger-garlic paste and sauté, adding two to three tablespoons water to avoid scorching. Add the marinated chicken with the marinade, mix

114

and sauté on medium heat for three to four minutes.

- Lower heat, cover the pan and cook for five minutes. Add the chopped coriander.

- Spread a layer of half the brown rice at the base of a wide and thick-bottomed pan. Sprinkle half quantity of following in this order: saffron-flavoured milk, rose petals, mint leaves, browned onions, screw pine essence, rose water and garam masala powder.

- Spread the layer of cooked chicken and cover with remaining brown rice.

- Sprinkle the remaining saffron-flavoured milk, rose petals, mint leaves, fried onions, screw pine essence, rose water and garam masala powder. Cover the pan with a tight-fitting lid and seal with the dough.

- Heat a non-stick tawa and place the pan on it. Cook on medium heat for about half an hour.

- Break seal just before serving. Serve hot with any raita of your choice.

70 Nizami Tarkari Biryani

This recipe from the Nizam's kitchen has a medley of fresh vegetables cooked with flavourful Basmati rice. Don't get overwhelmed with the array of spices - after all, it is something that is fit for royalty. It is delicious with raita and a few papads or chips.

INGREDIENTS

2½ cups Basmati rice, soaked

2 medium carrots, cut into diamonds and blanched

12-14 French beans, cut into diamonds and blanched

1 cup shelled green peas, blanched

150 grams cauliflower, separated into small florets, blanched

10 baby corns, cut into diamonds

Salt to taste

3 green cardamoms

2 one-inch cinnamon sticks

4 bay leaves

¼ cup oil

1 tablespoon caraway seeds

1 medium onion, chopped

1 tablespoon Garlic Paste (page 156)

½ tablespoon Ginger Paste (page 157)

5 crushed green cardamoms

4 crushed cloves

½ cup tomato purée

1 teaspoon turmeric powder

2 teaspoons coriander powder

3 teaspoons green cardamom powder

2 teaspoons red chilli powder

½ cup yogurt

3 one-inch ginger, cut into thin strips

5 green chillies, cut into thin strips

¾ cup + 2 tablespoons Browned Onions (page 156)

½ cup fresh mint

⅓ cup + ¼ cup chopped fresh coriander + for garnishing

2 tablespoons screw pine essence

A generous pinch of saffron

1¾ tablespoons butter

4 teaspoons cream

Whole-wheat dough to seal

METHOD

- Drain and cook the rice in five cups of water with salt, green cardamoms, one cinnamon stick and two bay leaves till three-fourth done.

- Drain, discard the whole spices and spread the rice out on a plate to cool.

- Heat the oil in a deep non-stick pan, add the caraway seeds and sauté till they change colour.

- Add the onion, garlic paste, ginger paste, crushed cardamoms, remaining cinnamon stick, crushed cloves, two bay leaves and sauté for five minutes.

- Add the tomato purée and one-fourth cup of water and sauté till oil rises to the surface.

- Add the turmeric powder, coriander powder, two teaspoons green cardamom powder, chilli powder, salt and yogurt and sauté for five minutes more.

- Add most of the ginger strips and green chilli strips and sauté for five minutes.

- Add the carrot, French beans, green peas, cauliflower, baby corns and sauté for ten minutes.

- Add one cup of water and half cup of browned

- onions and cook for ten minutes.

- Add remaining green cardamom powder, one-fourth cup fresh mint, one-third cup chopped fresh coriander and half cup water and cook for five minutes.

- Add the screw pine essence and mix. Spread the cooked rice over the vegetables.

- Sprinkle one-fourth cup of browned onions, remaining fresh mint, remaining ginger strips and one-fourth cup chopped fresh coriander.

- Mix the saffron with the butter and cream, add one-fourth cup of water and mix well.

- Sprinkle this mixture over the rice.

- Seal the pan with the dough.

- Cook on dum on low heat for ten to fifteen minutes.

- Serve hot garnished with the remaining chopped fresh coriander and two tablespoons of browned onions.

71 Anda Pulao

The Indian version of an egg fried rice which is a hot favourite with kids! So, some of the spices also come along for that ultimate aroma and taste. You really don't need anything else with it as it's best when eaten all by itself.

INGREDIENTS

1½ cups Basmati rice, soaked

4 eggs, hard-boiled and peeled

3 tablespoons oil

1 teaspoon cumin seeds

3-4 black peppercorns

2-3 cloves

2-3 green cardamoms

1 inch cinnamon

1 bay leaf

1 medium onion, sliced

1 tablespoon Ginger-Garlic-Green Chilli Paste (page 157)

1 teaspoon red chilli powder

1 teaspoon coriander powder

½ teaspoon Garam Masala Powder (page 156)

Salt to taste

2 tablespoons chopped fresh coriander

METHOD

- Heat the oil in a non-stick pan and shallow-fry the boiled eggs till light golden. Drain on absorbent paper.

- Add the cumin seeds to the same pan. When the cumin seeds change colour, add the peppercorns, cloves, green cardamoms, cinnamon, bay leaf and sauté till fragrant.

- Add the onion and sauté till light golden brown. Add the ginger-garlic-green chilli paste and sauté for a minute.

- Add the chilli powder, coriander powder, garam masala powder and sauté till the oil separates.

- Add three cups of water and bring it to a boil, add the salt and rice and mix well.

- Cover and cook till the rice is three-fourth done. Add the fried eggs and cook till the rice is done.

- Serve hot garnished with the chopped fresh coriander.

72 Kesari Seafood Pulao

Saffron with its characteristic flavour gives any rice preparation a touch of exotica. Saffron also combines well with seafood. So here we bring a unique dish combining all three...an effort that is well matched by the final full flavoured pulao that you put on the table!

INGREDIENTS

7-8 saffron threads

7-8 mussels

15-20 medium prawns, shelled and deveined

2 large pomfret fillets, cut into 1-inch pieces

1½ cups Basmati rice

Salt to taste

¾ cup yogurt, whisked

2 teaspoons Ginger Paste (page 157)

2 teaspoons Garlic Paste (page 156)

1 teaspoon Green Chilli Paste (page 157)

3 tablespoons oil + for deep-frying

4 medium onions, sliced

1 bay leaf

6-8 black peppercorns

2 black cardamoms

3-4 green cardamoms

1 star anise

2 inches cinnamon stick

½ teaspoon turmeric powder

1¼ teaspoons red chilli powder

2 teaspoons Garam Masala Powder (page 156)

1 tablespoon coriander powder

1 tablespoon lemon juice

2 tablespoons chopped fresh coriander

10-12 fresh mint leaves, hand torn

METHOD

- Soak rice in three cups of water for half an hour. Drain and set aside.

- Wash mussels and cook in salted boiling water for two minutes. Drain and set aside unshelled. Reserve the water.

- Place yogurt in a bowl, add half the ginger paste, half the garlic paste, half the green chilli paste and salt to taste. Mix well and marinate prawns and pomfret pieces in it.

- Heat sufficient oil in a kadai and deep-fry half the sliced onions till brown and crisp. Drain and place on absorbent paper.

- Heat three tablespoons oil in a non-stick pan and add bay leaf, peppercorns, black cardamoms, green cardamoms, star anise, cinnamon and the remaining half of the sliced onions. Sauté for two minutes.

- Add remaining ginger, garlic and green chilli pastes. Stir well and add rice.

- Sauté for two minutes and add water in which mussels were boiled.

- Add turmeric powder, chilli powder, garam masala powder, coriander powder and saffron threads.

- Mix well, add marinated prawns, fish and boiled mussels.

- Add salt, lemon juice, coriander and mint leaves. Stir and add fried onions.

Cover and cook on low heat for ten minutes.

- Remove from heat and allow to rest, covered, for five to ten minutes.

- Serve directly from the cooking pan at the dining table in order to retain maximum flavour.

73 Hyderabadi Dum Gosht Biryani

Dum cooking was revived in India in 1783 by Nawab Asaf-ud-Daulah, where food was par-cooked in large clay pots; the mouth of each pot covered with a clay saucer and sealed with a paste of flour to prevent the steam from escaping. Many people find it difficult to believe that uncooked mutton can be finished with half cooked rice. Yes, it is not only possible, but the end result will leave you completely amazed. One of the greatest ever treats from the royal kitchens of Hyderabad.

INGREDIENTS

500 grams mutton, cut into 1-inch pieces on the bone

2½ cups Basmati rice, washed and soaked for ½ hour

½ tablespoon Ginger Paste (page 157)

1 tablespoon Garlic Paste (page 156)

3 tablespoons Unripe Papaya Paste (page 158)

Salt to taste

½ tablespoon turmeric powder

1½ tablespoons red chilli powder

1½ tablespoons Biryani Masala (page 156)

¼ cup melted pure ghee

¼ cup + 2 tablespoons fresh mint, torn

4-5 green chillies, slit

1 inch ginger, cut into thin strips

½ cup yogurt, whisked

A few saffron threads

½ tablespoon warm milk

3 green cardamoms

3 cloves

1 black cardamom

1 inch cinnamon

2 tablespoons melted butter

2 tablespoons fresh cream

2 tablespoons Browned Onion (page 156)

Whole-wheat flour dough for sealing

METHOD

- In a bowl, mix together the mutton, ginger paste, garlic paste, papaya paste, salt, turmeric powder, half tablespoon chilli powder, half tablespoon biryani masala.

- Cover the bowl with a cling film and keep it in the refrigerator to marinate for four hours.

- Take the bowl out of the refrigerator and add the melted ghee and mix well.

- Add remaining biryani masala and chilli powder, one-fourth cup of mint leaves, salt, green chillies, ginger strips and yogurt and mix well. Set aside in the refrigerator to marinate for another hour.

- Soak the saffron in warm milk in a small bowl and set aside.

- Boil seven cups of water in a deep non-stick pan.

- Add the green cardamoms, cloves, black cardamom, cinnamon and salt and let it boil for a few minutes.

- Remove the whole spices.

- Drain the soaked rice and add and cook for five minutes. Drain well.

- Arrange the marinated mutton in another deep non-stick pan and top it with the rice.

- Mix the melted butter with the cream and pour this over the rice. Drizzle the saffron-flavoured milk and sprinkle browned onion and remaining mint leaves.

- Cover the pan with a lid and seal the edges with the flour dough.

- Cook on low heat for half an hour. Let it stand for five to ten minutes.

- Break open the seal and serve the biryani hot with your choice of raita.

74 Chicken Keema Pulao

How about serving an easy version of chicken biryani using keema instead of pieces of chicken?
The flavour is all encompassing and you will get repeat orders from your family for sure!

INGREDIENTS

200 grams chicken mince

1½ cups Basmati rice, soaked

1½ inch ginger

10-12 garlic cloves

4 tablespoons oil

2 cloves

½ inch cinnamon stick

2 green cardamoms

8-10 black peppercorns

1 teaspoon cumin seeds

3 medium onions, sliced

3-4 green chillies, slit

1 teaspoon red chilli powder

2 medium tomatoes, chopped

Salt to taste

15-20 fresh mint leaves, torn

2 tablespoons chopped fresh coriander

½ teaspoon Garam Masala Powder (page 156)

METHOD

• Grind ginger and garlic to a fine paste. Set aside.

• Heat oil in a non-stick pan, add cloves, cinnamon, green cardamoms, peppercorns, cumin seeds, onion and green chillies. Sauté till the onions begin to change colour.

• Add chicken mince and cook on high heat for four to five minutes. Add ginger-garlic paste, chilli powder, tomatoes, three cups of hot water, salt and Basmati rice.

• Mix lightly. Allow rice to come to a boil on high heat. Cover the pan and cook on low heat for twelve to fifteen minutes.

• Add mint leaves, chopped coriander and garam masala powder. Cover and further cook for five to seven minutes. Remove from heat and serve hot.

75 Tawa **Roti**

The quintessential Indian flatbread prepared on a griddle or a tawa. Tastes great with all Indian curries and sabzis, or just spread some butter or ghee on it, top with some jaggery, roll and indulge! Trust me, it tastes heavenly!

INGREDIENTS

2 cups whole-wheat flour + for dusting

Salt to taste

Oil, as required

METHOD

- Mix the flour, salt and one teaspoon of oil in a parat. Add one cup water, little by little and knead into soft dough. Apply little oil on the dough, cover and rest for fifteen to twenty minutes.

- Divide the dough into twelve equal portions and shape them into balls. Dust them lightly with dry flour and roll into round rotis.

- Heat a non-stick tawa. Place a roti on it and cook for two minutes on medium heat.

- Flip and cook again on the other side for two minutes.

- Remove the roti from the tawa, apply a little oil and serve hot.

76 Paneer Kulcha

A filling cottage cheese-stuffed bread that can also
be served as a starter when cut into small squares.

INGREDIENTS

200 grams cottage cheese, grated

½ medium onion, finely chopped

Salt to taste

½ teaspoon red chilli powder

Onion seeds, as required

Butter for serving

1 tablespoon oil + for greasing

Kulcha Dough

2 cups refined flour

½ teaspoon baking powder

¼ teaspoon soda bicarbonate

½ teaspoon salt

1 teaspoon sugar

½ cup milk

1 tablespoon yogurt

METHOD

- To knead the kulcha dough, sift the flour together with the baking powder, soda bicarbonate and salt into a bowl. Add the sugar, milk and yogurt. Knead well into a medium soft dough.

- Apply one tablespoon oil on the dough, cover with a damp cloth and set aside for one hour.

- Mix the onion with the cottage cheese in a deep bowl. Add the salt and chilli powder and mix well.

- Grease your palms with a little oil and take a portion of the dough on one palm.

- Spread the dough with your fingers, place a portion of the stuffing in the centre, gather the edges and seal it well to enclose the stuffing

completely and shape them into pedas. Make the other pedas.

- Put a little oil on each peda, and press lightly. Set them aside for fifteen minutes.

- Sprinkle a few onion seeds on each peda. Moisten your left hand with water, place a peda over it and spread, using both hands, into a round kulcha.

- Heat a non-stick tawa. Place a kulcha over it with the side moistened with water facing down. Cover and cook till the underside is golden. Flip, cover and cook till the other side is equally golden.

- Serve hot with salad and raita.

77 Puri

It is very common that when these crispy puris land on the plate, they get devoured within minutes. Still if you get a chance to reserve some, have it with kale chane and a bit of hot halwa on the side to complete the triangle! This makes quite a good tiffin snack too.

INGREDIENTS

1 cup whole-wheat flour

2 tablespoons semolina

Salt to taste

1 teaspoon oil + for deep-frying

METHOD

- Combine the flour, semolina and salt in a bowl. Heat one teaspoon of oil and add; mix well and knead into stiff dough with sufficient water.

- Cover and set aside for twenty to twenty-five minutes.

- Heat sufficient oil in a kadai.

- Divide the dough into small equal portions and shape them into balls. Apply a little oil to each ball and roll into a puri.

- Slide each puri into the hot oil and deep-fry, pressing lightly, till well-puffed and golden.

- Drain on absorbent paper. Serve hot.

78 Phulka

When fluffed phulkas or rotis are put on your plate, you simply have to watch them for a while before breaking off a piece and putting it into your mouth along with a dal or a sabzi. Too comforting, isn't it?

INGREDIENTS

2 cups whole-wheat flour + for dusting

Salt to taste

1 teaspoon of oil + for greasing

METHOD

- Combine the flour, salt and one teaspoon of oil in a parat.

- Add one cup of water, little by little, and knead into soft dough. Apply little oil on the dough, cover and rest for fifteen to twenty minutes.

- Divide the dough into eight equal portions and shape them into balls.

- Dust each of them lightly with dry flour and roll out into thin rotis.

- Heat a non-stick tawa. Place a roti on it and cook for one minute on medium heat.

- Flip and cook again on the other side for two minutes.

- Remove from the tawa, place the lesser cooked side on open flame and let it puff.

- Serve hot.

79 Lachcha Parantha

The lachcha parantha, also known as multi-layered Indian bread, is flaky and deliciously fragile. It is a bit tricky to make, but very tasty, with several crisp layers. Perfect for eating with the highly spiced and flavourful kababs, curries and stews of the north.

INGREDIENTS

2½ cups whole-wheat flour + for dusting

½ cup refined flour

Salt to taste

8 teaspoons pure ghee + for shallow-frying

METHOD

- Combine both the flours with salt and one and a half cups of water in a bowl and knead into soft dough.

- Cover with a damp cloth and rest for about fifteen minutes. Divide into eight equal portions. Roll out each portion into a thin chapati.

- Spread one teaspoon ghee on it and dust with a little flour. Make small pleats and then roll into a round and rest for ten minutes. Roll out each round into a slightly thick parantha of five-to six- inch diameter.

- Heat a non-stick tawa and place a parantha on it. Drizzle with a little ghee, turn it over and drizzle some more ghee and cook till both the sides are golden brown.

- Crush lightly with your hands to open out the layers and serve hot.

80 Carrot **Tomato** Puri

Puris have been transformed into power houses with nutritious fresh vegetable juice used to knead the dough instead of water in this recipe. Tomato purée lends an appealing colour and flavour.

INGREDIENTS

2 cups whole-wheat flour

2 medium carrots, grated

2 medium ripe red tomatoes, puréed

3 tablespoons oil + for deep-frying

Salt to taste

1 teaspoon red chilli powder

METHOD

- Extract juice of carrots and mix with tomato purée. Strain.

- Place flour in a deep bowl. Add three tablespoons oil, salt and chilli powder.

- Knead into a medium stiff dough using the carrot-tomato mixture.

- Divide into lemon-sized portions and shape into balls. Roll out into small puris.

- Heat sufficient oil in a non-stick kadai and deep-fry puris. Drain on absorbent paper.

- Serve hot.

81 Makki Di Roti

Hot and buttery, delicious on its own,
superb with sarson da saag!

INGREDIENTS

1½ cups cornmeal

¼ cup whole-wheat flour
(optional)

Salt to taste

Fresh homemade white
butter, as required

METHOD

- Add salt and flour to the
  cornmeal and mix well.

- Add warm water and
  knead to make a medium-
  soft dough. Divide into
  eight equal portions and
  shape into balls.

- Pat each ball between
  moistened palms to
  make a roti of medium
  thickness.

- Alternatively, roll out each
  ball between the folds of
  a greased plastic sheet.

- Heat a non-stick tawa
  and place a roti on it.
  Cook on medium heat till
  one side is half-done. Flip
  and spread some white
  butter over the surface.

- Flip and spread some
  more butter on the other
  side. Cook till both sides
  are golden brown.

- Serve hot with a dollop of
  white butter.

82 Aloo Matar Parantha

The name is a bit misleading – the paranthe are not made with the aloo matar, the popular Punjabi dish. But yes, the stuffing for these paranthe is indeed a delicious mix of potatoes and green peas with simple spices.

INGREDIENTS

3 medium potatoes, boiled, peeled and mashed

½ cup shelled green peas, boiled and mashed

2 cups whole-wheat flour + for dusting

Salt to taste

2½ tablespoons oil + for frying

1 teaspoon dried pomegranate seeds, crushed

½ teaspoon Ginger-Green Chilli Paste (page 157)

1 teaspoon dried mango powder

1 teaspoon Chaat Masala (page 156)

½ teaspoon red chilli powder

1 teaspoon crushed dried mint leaves

Butter, for serving

METHOD

- Sift the flour with salt in a bowl. Add two and half tablespoons of oil and three-fourth cup water and knead into a smooth and semi-soft dough.

- Cover with a damp cloth and set aside for fifteen minutes.

- Mix the potatoes, peas, crushed dried pomegranate seeds, ginger-green chilli paste, dried mango powder, chaat masala, chilli powder, mint leaves and salt to taste. Divide into eight equal portions

- Divide dough into eight equal portions and shape into small balls. Roll out each ball into small square. Place a portion of the filling in the centre, bring in the edges to form a neat square. Press lightly and roll out, dusting with a little dry flour if needed, into round shaped parantha.

- Heat a non-stick tawa; place a parantha on it and cook on low heat for three minutes. Flip it over and drizzle some oil all around.

- Flip it over again and drizzle little oil all around again.

- Cook on high heat till golden brown. Serve hot with butter.

83 Appam

If appams are around, can a stew be far behind? Serve these lacy confections with a Malabar Chemeen Kari instead and you will begin to discover delicious combinations you have never explored.

INGREDIENTS

1 cup rice

1 cup parboiled rice

¼ cup coconut water

Salt to taste

¾ cup grated coconut

¼ teaspoon baking powder

Oil for greasing

METHOD

- Soak both types of rice together in four cups of water for two to three hours.

- Drain and grind to a smooth paste adding the coconut water, as required.

- Add the salt, stir well and set aside in a warm place to ferment for at least thirty-six hours.

- Soak the grated coconut in one and a half cups of warm water; grind and extract thick milk.

- Add the coconut milk to the fermented batter to dilute it to a thick and creamy consistency. Mix in the baking powder and adjust the salt.

- Heat an appam tawa; brush it with a little oil. Pour in one ladleful of batter and tilt the tawa all round to spread the batter.

- The edges should be thin and the excess batter should collect in the centre at the bottom.

- Cover with a thick heavy lid and cook over medium heat for two to three minutes.

- Check to see if the sides start leaving the tawa.

- The edges of the appam should be crisp and thin and the centre soft and spongy.

- Serve hot with a spicy curry.

Chef's Tip: Traditionally fresh toddy is used to ferment appam batter. In the above recipe, the coconut water acts as the fermenting agent. A special cast iron appam tawa is used to make appam. However, you may use a small non-stick kadai.

84 Anda Parantha

This combination of eggs and flours makes for a filling breakfast. Having eggs for breakfast keeps those hunger pangs at bay longer, helping you stay away from mid-morning snacks.

INGREDIENTS

5 eggs

1 cup refined flour

1 cup whole-wheat flour

Salt to taste

2 green chillies, finely chopped

½ teaspoon carom seeds

2 tablespoons butter

5 tablespoons oil

2 tablespoons finely chopped fresh coriander

METHOD

- Sieve together both the flour and one teaspoon salt into a bowl.

- Break four eggs into a bowl and whisk with the salt.

- Make a soft dough with the mixed flours, green chillies, carom seeds, one egg and approximately three-fourth cup of water.

- Cover with a damp cloth and set aside for an hour. Divide the dough into four equal portions. Roll out each portion into a round of four-inch diameter. Spread a little butter on each round, sprinkle a little flour and fold into four.

- Roll out again on a floured surface into six-inch diameter parantha.

- Heat a non-stick tawa, and place a parantha on it. When one side is half done, turn over and spread some egg and some chopped coriander on the upper side. Pour a little oil round the edges and turn over.

- Apply some egg and chopped coriander on the other side and shallow-fry till both the sides are evenly golden.

- Serve hot with your choice of pickle.

Chapter 6
Accompaniments

85 Sookhi Dal Amritsari

A must try preparation for all dal lovers. Very popular in Punjab, perhaps that is the reason it is called sookhi dal amritsari. It is tangy, it is spicy, it is dry and it is very delicious. Ideal to pack in tiffin box since you need not worry that it will spill.

INGREDIENTS

1 cup skinless split black gram, soaked

Salt to taste

½ teaspoon turmeric powder

3 one-inch ginger, cut into thin strips

4 tablespoons oil

A pinch of asafoetida

1½ teaspoons cumin seeds

2 medium onions, chopped

4-5 green chillies, chopped

3 medium tomatoes, chopped

1 teaspoon red chilli powder

¾ teaspoon Garam Masala Powder (page 156)

2 tablespoons chopped fresh coriander

4 teaspoons lemon juice

METHOD

- Place the black gram, three cups of water, salt, turmeric powder and half the ginger in a deep non-stick pan.

- Bring the mixture to a boil on high heat, then reduce heat and cook till just done.

- Heat the oil in another non-stick pan.

- Add the asafoetida, cumin seeds, onion and sauté till onion is light brown.

- Add the remaining ginger, green chillies and tomatoes and sauté.

- Add the chilli powder and sauté till the oil rises to the surface.

- Strain the cooked black gram and add to the masala. Mix, add the salt, garam masala powder, chopped fresh coriander and lemon juice.

- Cook for two more minutes. Serve hot.

86 Coconut Chutney

Dosas and idlis cannot be thought of without this amazing chutney, forget eating them alone! This is a definite must for all the popular South Indian breakfast items.

INGREDIENTS

1 cup grated fresh coconut

Salt to taste

1 tablespoon oil

1 whole dried red chilli, broken into 3 pieces

¼ teaspoon mustard seeds

½ teaspoon skinless split black gram

5-6 curry leaves

METHOD

- Use only the white part of the grated coconut, discarding any brown bits.

- Grind coconut with very little water. Add salt to taste and mix well. The consistency of the chutney should be thick.

- Heat oil in a small non-stick pan. Add broken red chillies, mustard seed and split black gram.

- When the seeds splutter and dal turns light brown, add curry leaves. Add the fried spices to the ground coconut.

- Mix thoroughly and serve as an accompaniment with idlis or dosas.

Chef's Tip: You can add ginger or garlic, or both to enhance the taste.

87 Gujarati Kadhi

For some time after I got married to Alyona, I used to enjoy this kadhi as a soup!
Now I have learnt the traditional way, served piping hot with steamed rice. You can
make the meal healthier by having steamed brown rice instead of white rice.

INGREDIENTS

¼ cup gram flour

2 cups yogurt

1 lemon-sized piece of
jaggery, grated

2 green chillies, chopped

Salt to taste

2 tablespoons oil

½ teaspoon mustard seeds

½ teaspoon cumin seeds

8-10 curry leaves

2 whole dried red
chillies, broken

3-4 cloves

1 inch cinnamon stick

⅛ teaspoon asafoetida

METHOD

- Whisk together the gram flour and yogurt
  to make a smooth mixture. Add four cups of
  water and mix well.

- Combine the yogurt mixture, jaggery and
  green chillies.

- Cook, stirring continuously, till the kadhi
  attains medium consistency. Add the salt
  to taste.

- Heat the oil in a small non-stick pan and
  add the mustard seeds, cumin seeds, curry
  leaves, dried red chillies, cloves, cinnamon
  and asafoetida.

- When the seeds splutter, add it to the kadhi
  and mix well.

- Serve hot.

88 Dal Tadka

Dal is, perhaps, one of the most ubiquitous part of Indian menu. In most homes dal in some form or the other is cooked everyday. The seasoning and tempering may vary, but it is dal which is enjoyed by most of us daily.

INGREDIENTS

1 cup split pigeon peas, soaked

¾ teaspoon turmeric powder

Salt to taste

2 tablespoons oil

2 tablespoons ghee

1 teaspoon cumin seeds

15-20 garlic cloves, finely chopped

¼ teaspoon asafoetida

½ teaspoon red chilli powder

½ teaspoon dried mango powder

METHOD

- Drain the pigeon peas and cook under pressure with two and half cups of water, one-fourth teaspoon turmeric powder and salt till the pressure is released three times.

- Heat the oil and ghee in a non-stick pan. Add the cumin seeds and sauté till light brown.

- Add the garlic and sauté till golden. Add the asafoetida and sauté.

- Add the boiled pigeon peas and enough water to get the consistency you require. Mix well.

- Add the chilli powder, remaining turmeric powder, salt and dried mango powder and mix well. Simmer for two to three minutes.

- Serve hot with steamed rice.

89 Maa **Chole** Di Dal

Urad dal and chana dal perfectly blended, cooked in ghee with spices to give you a hearty preparation. A favourite of most Punjabis, it tastes great with paranthas or naans or even plain steamed rice.

INGREDIENTS

½ cup split black gram with skin

½ cup split Bengal gram

Salt to taste

¼ teaspoon turmeric powder

1 inch ginger, chopped

3 green chillies, chopped

2-3 tablespoons pure ghee

1 tablespoon butter

1 teaspoon cumin seeds

1 medium onion, chopped

2 medium tomatoes, chopped

½ teaspoon red chilli powder

2 tablespoons chopped fresh coriander

METHOD

- Mix both the gram, wash and soak in four cups of water for an hour. Drain.

- Place the soaked gram in a non-stick pan with four cups of water, salt, turmeric powder, half each of ginger and green chillies.

- Cover and cook on low heat till the gram are tender.

- Stir well with a ladle to make a homogeneous mixture of the gram without mashing them.

- Heat ghee and butter in a non-stick pan.

- Add the cumin seeds, remaining green chillies and remaining ginger.

- Stir and add the onion and sauté till the onion turns light brown.

- Add the tomatoes and sauté till the tomatoes soften.

- Add the chilli powder and sauté for half a minute.

- Add the seasoning to the dal and mix. Simmer for a few minutes and serve hot garnished with the chopped fresh coriander.

90 Mixed Vegetable Raita

Raitas make an excellent accompaniment to any fiery dish – be it biryani, pulao, vegetarian or non-vegetarian curry. The yogurt soothes the tongue and intestines and eases off the burning sensation that is left behind by the hot spices. Vegetables add their own nutrition in this raita.

INGREDIENTS

1 medium cucumber, finely chopped

1 medium tomato, finely chopped

1 small onion, finely chopped

2 cups yogurt, whisked

1 teaspoon Roasted Cumin Powder (158)

½ teaspoon red chilli powder

1 teaspoon sugar

Salt to taste

2 green chillies, finely chopped

¾ teaspoon Chaat Masala (page 156)

2 tablespoons chopped fresh coriander

5-6 fresh mint leaves, hand torn

A fresh coriander sprig, for garnishing

METHOD

- Mix together the cucumber, tomato, onion, cumin powder, one-fourth teaspoon chilli powder, sugar, salt, green chillies and half the chaat masala in a bowl.

- Add the chopped coriander, torn fresh mint leaves and mix well. Add the yogurt and mix well.

- Sprinkle the remaining chaat masala and remaining chilli powder and garnish with a sprig of fresh coriander. Serve chilled with biryani.

Chapter 7
Desserts

91 **Pineapple** Sheera

Soft and smooth sheera can be given an interesting texture with little pieces of fresh pineapple that burst into sweet flavour with every bite adding amazing deliciousness to the dessert! Do try it once and see how the family will want more!

INGREDIENTS

1½ cups chopped fresh pineapple

1 cup semolina

1 cup + 3 tablespoons pure ghee

A pinch of saffron threads

1 cup sugar

5-6 cashew nuts, chopped

5-6 almonds, chopped

METHOD

- Heat one cup ghee in a deep non-stick kadai.

- Add the semolina and sauté, stirring continuously, till fragrant and golden brown. Add the saffron and mix. Add the pineapple and cook for two or three more minutes.

- Stir in two cups of water; cover and cook on medium heat for three minutes.

- Add the sugar and keep stirring till all the moisture evaporates and the semolina is cooked completely. Add the remaining pure ghee, cashew nuts and almonds and mix well.

- Serve hot.

92 Kesar **Pista** Phirni

This legacy of Mughal cuisine has me enthralled at all times. I find this silky smooth dessert particularly enticing as it leaves me with no feelings of guilt! And moreover, I love looking at it too as its simply beautiful.

INGREDIENTS

A few threads of saffron

10-12 pistachios, blanched, peeled and sliced

1 litre skimmed milk

3 tablespoons coarse rice flour

¾ teaspoon Green Cardamom Powder (page 157)

9 tablespoons sugar

METHOD

- Bring the milk to a boil in a deep non-stick pan. Reduce the heat and simmer, stirring continuously till it reduces to half.

- Add the rice flour to the milk and stir well to prevent lumps from forming. Bring the mixture to a boil. When it starts to thicken, reduce the heat and simmer for a couple of minutes, stirring continuously. Add the cardamom powder and saffron and mix well.

- When the mixture attains a thick custard-like consistency, add the sugar. Cook, stirring continuously, till the sugar dissolves.

- Pour the mixture into four individual earthenware bowls while still warm. Sprinkle sliced pistachios and refrigerate for at least two hours. Serve chilled.

93 Santra **Rawa** Malpua

Sweet and small and exotically orange in flavour! Malpua, lightly fried in ghee and dipped in sugar syrup, that's the dessert of the day for you to make and please your family with...

INGREDIENTS

10 tablespoons orange concentrate

5 tablespoons semolina

5 tablespoons refined flour

½ cup sugar

¾ cup rabdi + for serving

¼ cup milk

2 tablespoons yogurt

Pure ghee for shallow-frying

METHOD

- Cook sugar with two tablespoons water to make a syrup.

- Add half of the orange concentrate and mix well. Continue to cook on low heat for three to four minutes. Keep it warm.

- Mix the flour, semolina, remaining orange concentrate and rabdi in a bowl.

- Add the milk and mix to make a smooth batter. Add the yogurt and mix well.

- Heat a non-stick pan, drizzle a little ghee, pour a spoonful of batter and spread it slightly.

- Make some more such malpua, keeping a little distance between each. Cook on medium heat drizzling with little ghee around the sides.

- When the underside is light golden brown, turn them over and cook till the other side is also done. Drain the malpua on absorbent paper.

- Remove the sugar syrup from the heat and immerse the malpua in the syrup for ten to twelve minutes. Serve hot.

- Alternatively, serve malpua with rabdi or ice cream.

94 Coconut Karanji

Yummy filling of cardamom flavoured coconut in neatly done pastry dough, deep-fried and served.
Believe it or not, it's hard to wait for even the oil to drain on the kitchen towel! And once you break
it and put a morsel in your mouth, you seldom would want to stop at one!
Just run a few more miles to knock-off those extra calories.

INGREDIENTS

Pastry

1 cup refined flour

1½ tablespoons semolina

4 tablespoons Ghee (page 156) + for deep-frying

¼ cup milk

Stuffing

1 cup grated coconut

15-20 raisins, chopped

1 cup powdered sugar

½ teaspoon Green Cardamom Powder (page 157)

METHOD

- Sieve the refined flour into a bowl. Add the semolina and four tablespoons of ghee and mix with fingertips till mixture resembles breadcrumbs. Knead into semi-soft dough with milk and sufficient water.

- Cover the dough with a damp cloth and set it aside for half an hour.

- For stuffing, roast the coconut in a non-stick pan till lightly browned.

- Add the raisins, powdered sugar, green cardamom powder and mix well. Let it cool.

- Knead the dough once again and divide into twelve small balls.

- Roll out each ball into a circle, place it in a greased karanji mould. Place a small portion of the prepared filling in the hollow.

- Apply a little water on edges, close the mould and press firmly.

- Heat sufficient ghee in a kadai and deep-fry the karanjis, two at a time, on medium heat till crisp and golden brown.

- Drain on absorbent paper and allow to cool before storing in an air-tight container.

95 Chocolate Gujiya

A surprise filled mithai! Chocolate filling is the least
expected when anyone bites into it! Is bound to delight!

INGREDIENTS

Pastry

2 cups refined flour

3 tablespoons oil
+ for greasing and
deep-frying

Filling

15 cashew nuts, chopped

15 almonds, blanched
and chopped

20 raisins

A pinch of nutmeg powder

¼ teaspoon Green
Cardamom Powder
(page 157)

½ cup powdered sugar

1 cup grated dark chocolate

METHOD

- For the pastry, sift refined flour and rub in three tablespoons of oil.

- Add cold water as needed and knead into a stiff dough. Cover with a damp cloth and set aside.

- For the filling, mix cashew nuts, almonds, raisins, nutmeg powder and cardamom powder and mix well.

- Add powdered sugar and grated chocolate and mix well. Divide into twelve portions.

- Grease the palms of your hands with oil and divide dough into twelve portions and shape into balls. Grease a gujiya mould.

- Roll out dough balls into small puris, place it on the mould and press lightly.

- Place a portion of the stuffing in the hollow portion.

- Apply a little water on the edges, close mould and press firmly. Open mould and remove extra dough.

- Keep gujiyas covered with a damp cloth. Use up all the dough and stuffing in a similar manner to make more gujiyas.

- Heat sufficient oil in a non-stick kadai and deep-fry gujiyas on medium heat till golden brown. Drain on absorbent paper.

- Let them cool slightly before serving, as the stuffing inside may be very hot.

Note: *If you do not have a mould, gujiyas can still be prepared. Roll out puris, cut with a katori (approx. of four-five inch diameter) to get a proper round shape. Place a portion of stuffing on one half, lightly moisten edges with water and fold the other half over the stuffing. Press edges firmly and seal them using a fork.*

96 Ukdiche Modak

Lord Ganesh loves these little steamed dumplings made of a translucent rice flour pastry stuffed with a sweetened mixture of coconut and jaggery. It's a sure-shot art to shape these into perfect ones. But once done, they are pure divine!

INGREDIENTS

1½ cups Basmati rice flour

A pinch of salt

1 teaspoon oil + for greasing

Filling

1½ cups grated fresh coconut

1 cup grated jaggery

1 tablespoon roasted poppy seeds

A pinch of Green Cardamom Powder (page 157)

A pinch of nutmeg powder

METHOD

- Boil one and one-fourth cups of water with salt and one teaspoon oil in a deep non-stick pan.

- Reduce heat, and add the rice flour in a steady flow, stirring continuously to prevent lumps from forming. Cover the pan with a deep lid and pour some water into the lid. Cook on low heat for three minutes.

- Remove the lid, sprinkle some cold water on the rice flour and cover again with the lid with water in it; cook for another three minutes. Repeat this process twice more. Take the pan off the heat and keep it covered for two minutes.

- Transfer the mixture to a large parat; grease the palms of your hands with oil and knead the dough till completely smooth and pliable. The dough should not stick to your palms. Rest the dough covered with a damp cloth.

- For the stuffing, combine the coconut and jaggery in a non-stick pan and cook on medium heat for one or two minutes till light golden brown. Make sure that you do not overcook the mixture. Add the roasted poppy seeds, cardamom powder and nutmeg powder and mix well. Remove from heat and set aside to cool. Divide the coconut mixture into twelve equal portions.

- Divide the dough into twelve equal portions and shape them into balls. Grease the palms of your hands and spread each ball to form a three-inch wide round. Press the edges of the round to reduce the thickness.

- Place a portion of the stuffing in the centre; pleat the edges of the dough and gather them together to form a bundle. Pinch to seal the edges at the top. Heat sufficient water in a steamer. Place the modak on a perforated plate, fit it in the steamer and steam for ten to twelve minutes.

- Serve hot modak with pure ghee.

97 **Shahi** Tukre

As the name shahi suggests, this is a dessert from the times of royalty. It is simple, easy to make and also gives you the scope to make variations. Like I did, by preparing a stuffed version, which became an instant hit. I personally enjoy it when served warm in winters.

INGREDIENTS

6 white bread slices

2 tablespoons pure Ghee
(page 156)

2 cups milk

4 tablespoons sugar

3-4 saffron threads, crushed

1 cup crumbled Khoya/Mawa
(page 157)

½ teaspoon Green
Cardamom Powder
(page 157)

15 cashew nuts, chopped

1 tablespoon cudpahnuts

A few drops rose essence

8-10 almonds, chopped

1 sheet edible silver foil

A few rose petals

METHOD

- Preheat the oven to 180⁰C/350⁰F/Gas Mark 4.

- Remove the crust from bread slices and cut each slice diagonally into two.

- Arrange them on a baking tray, brush ghee on them and toast them in the preheated oven for twenty minutes or till they become golden and crisp.

- Meanwhile heat the milk with sugar and saffron in a non-stick pan.

- Reduce heat and continue to simmer for twelve to fifteen minutes or till it is reduced to three-fourth its original volume.

- Add the crumbled khoya, cardamom powder and

half the cashew nuts and half the cudpahnuts.

- Remove from the heat and set aside to cool. Add the rose essence.

- Take the bread out of the oven and spoon thickened milk on them. Sprinkle the almonds, remaining cashew nuts and

cudpahnuts and bake for further fifteen minutes.

- Decorate with rose petals and silver foil and serve warm or cold.

98 Apple Rabdi

Grated apples add a new dimension to this delicate milk delicacy. But remember to peel and grate the apples just before adding to the reduced milk. Otherwise, it will get discoloured and spoil the appearance of the rabdi.

INGREDIENTS

3 medium apples

1 litre milk

4 tablespoons sugar

¼ teaspoon Green Cardamom Powder (page 157)

8-10 almonds, blanched and sliced

8-10 pistachios, blanched and sliced

METHOD

- Pour the milk into a wide non-stick pan and bring it to a boil. Simmer till it gets reduced to half the original quantity.

- Add the sugar and cook on low heat, stirring continuously.

- Peel and grate two apples and add to the reduced milk and mix.

- Cook for three to four minutes. Add the cardamom powder, almonds and pistachios and mix well.

- Pour into a serving bowl. Thinly slice the remaining apple and arrange them all around the dish.

- Serve hot or cold.

99 Churma Laddoo

A traditional Rajasthani sweet, churma laddoo is made during festivals. It is quite nutritious too as it is made with whole-wheat flour and jaggery but that does not mean you just gorge on them. Remember there is plenty of ghee too. So enjoy them and then, you know what you have to!

INGREDIENTS

2 cups coarse whole-wheat flour

4 tablespoons Ghee (page 156) + for deep-frying

¾ cup grated jaggery

¼ cup (30 grams) powdered sugar

1 teaspoon Green Cardamom Powder (page 157)

1 teaspoon nutmeg powder

Poppy seeds, as required

METHOD

- Place the flour in a bowl; add two tablespoons of hot ghee and gently rub it in with your fingertips.

- Add sufficient warm water and knead into stiff dough.

- Divide the dough into four equal portions and shape into muthia (oval-shaped croquettes).

- Heat sufficient ghee in a non-stick kadai and deep-fry the muthia till golden brown.

- Drain on absorbent paper, break into smaller pieces and set aside to cool.

- When completely cool, grind the muthia to a powder. Pass the powder through a sieve.

- Grind the residue remaining in the sieve to a fine powder and add to the sifted powder.

- Heat two tablespoons of ghee in a non-stick pan. Add the jaggery and cook, stirring, till it melts.

- Remove from the heat and add the sifted muthia flour and mix well. Add the powdered sugar and mix.

- Add the cardamom powder and nutmeg powder, and mix well.

- Divide the mixture into sixteen equal portions and shape each portion into a laddoo.

- Roll the laddoo in the poppy seeds. Cool and store in an air-tight container.

100 **Atta** Ka Halwa

Indian dessert at its best – coarse whole-wheat flour sautéed in ghee till golden, sweetened and flavoured with cardamom. Easy and worth the try as the taste is simply blissful.

INGREDIENTS

1 cup coarse whole-wheat flour

1 cup Ghee (page 156)

1 cup sugar

A pinch of Green Cardamom Powder (page 157)

METHOD

- Boil four cups of water in a deep non-stick pan.

- Heat the ghee in another non-stick pan; add the flour and sauté for twelve to fifteen minutes or till golden.

- Add the sugar and cardamom powder and mix well.

- Add the boiling water and cook on high heat for three to four minutes or till all the water is absorbed.

- Transfer into a serving bowl and serve hot.

Annexure

Biryani Masala

Grind together 3-inch cinnamon, 15 cloves, 25-30 black peppercorns, 30 green cardamoms, 3 black cardamoms, 4 star anise, 2 tablespoons caraway seeds, 8 bay leaves, 2 tablespoons coriander seeds, 3 dried red chillies, 2 mace blades, ¼ teaspoon nutmeg powder. Store in an air-tight container.

Browned Onion/Browned Onion Paste

Peel, wash and slice onions. Heat sufficient oil in a kadai and deep-fry the onions till golden and crisp. Drain onto an absorbent paper. Use as required. To make browned onion paste, process the browned onion in a blender to make a fine paste.

Chaat Masala

Dry-roast 4 tablespoons coriander seeds, 2 teaspoons cumin seeds and 1 teaspoon carom seeds separately. Cool and powder them with 2-3 whole dried red chillies, 3 tablespoons black salt and ½ teaspoon citric acid. Mix in 1 teaspoon dried mango powder, 1 tablespoon salt and 1 teaspoon white/black pepper powder. Store in an air-tight container.

Coconut Milk

Process 1 cup grated fresh coconut in a blender with ¼ cup warm water. Pass the ground coconut through a piece of muslin or strainer pressing firmly to extract all the juice, or first milk. Add a ¼ cup of warm water to the strained coconut to get the second, thinner milk from the same solids.

Garam Masala Powder

Dry-roast 10-12 mace blades, 8-10 one-inch cinnamon sticks, 25 cloves, 25 green cardamoms, 10-12 black cardamoms, 2 nutmegs, 8-10 bay leaves, 8 teaspoons cumin seeds and 20-24 black peppercorns lightly. Cool, grind to a fine powder and store in an air-tight container.

Garlic Paste

Grind 55 peeled garlic cloves with 8 tablespoons water to a smooth paste. Transfer it in an air-tight container and store it in the refrigerator.

Ghee

Heat 2½ cups white butter in a deep non-stick pan. Once the butter melts, reduce heat to low and simmer, stirring frequently, so that it does not scorch. Cook for 30 minutes or till it turns light brown and the residue settles down. Remove from heat and cool. Strain into an air-tight jar and let it cool completely. Cover and store.

Ginger Paste

Grind 7½-inch peeled and roughly chopped ginger with 3 tablespoons water to a smooth paste. Put it in an air-tight container and store it in the refrigerator.

Ginger-Garlic Paste

Peel and roughly chop 3-inch ginger and 20 garlic cloves and grind them with 4 tablespoons water to a smooth paste. Transfer it in an air-tight container and store it in the refrigerator.

Ginger-Garlic-Green Chilli Paste

Peel and roughly chop 3-inch ginger and 20 garlic cloves and grind them with 12 roughly chopped green chillies and 4 tablespoons water to a smooth paste.

Ginger-Green Chilli Paste

Place peeled and chopped 3-inch ginger and roughly chopped 15 green chillies in a blender jar. Add 5 tablespoons water and grind to a smooth paste.

Green Cardamon Powder

Peel 100 grams green cardamoms and take out the seeds. Dry-roast the seeds till fragrant. Remove from heat, cool and grind into a fine powder. Store in an air-tight jar and use as required.

Green Chilli Paste

Grind 12 roughly chopped green chillies with 2 tablespoons water to a smooth paste.

Green Chutney

Grind together 1 cup fresh coriander, ½ cup fresh mint, 2-3 green chillies, black salt to taste, ¼ teaspoon sugar and 1 tablespoon lemon juice to a smooth paste using a little water if required. Transfer to a bowl and use as required.

Khoya/Mawa

Boil 1 litre full cream buffalo milk in a deep thick-bottomed non-stick pan. Reduce the heat and simmer, stirring continuously, till the milk reduces and forms a thick lump. It is very important to stir continuously and not allow the cream to form on the surface because this will affect the texture of the khoya.

Mint Chutney

Grind 5 cups mint leaves, 3 cups coriander leaves, 10 green chillies, 3 onions, and 3-inch ginger to a fine paste, adding a little water if required. Stir in 1 tablespoon lemon juice, salt and pomegranate seed powder to taste.

Roasted Cumin Powder

Dry-roast 40 grams cumin seeds till lightly coloured. Remove from heat, cool completely and grind to a fine powder.

Sweet Date and Tamarind Chutney

Stone 15-20 dates and chop roughly. Dry-roast 2 teaspoons cumin seeds and ¼ teaspoon fennel seeds. Cool slightly and grind to a powder. Mix together dates, ½ cup grated jaggery, 1 cup tamarind pulp, cumin and fennel powder, 2 teaspoons red chilli powder, 1 teaspoon dried ginger powder, 1 teaspoon black salt, salt and four cups water. Cook on medium heat till it comes to a boil, reduce heat and continue to cook for 6-8 minutes. Cool and use as required.

Tamarind Pulp

Soak 75 grams tamarind in 100 ml warm water for 10-15 minutes. Grind to a smooth paste and strain to remove any fibres. Store in an air-tight container in the refrigerator.

Unripe Papaya Paste

Peel and seed 300 grams unripe papaya, cut into ½-inch cubes and put into a blender jar. Add ¼ cup water and grind to a smooth paste.

Vegetable Stock

Heat 5 cups water in a deep non-stick pan. Add 1 medium sliced onion, ½ medium sliced carrot, 3-inch chopped celery stalk, 2 crushed garlic cloves, 1 bay leaf, 5-6 black peppercorns and 2-3 cloves and bring the mixture to a boil. Reduce heat and simmer for 30 minutes. Strain the stock, cool and store in the refrigerator till further use.

Glossary

English	Hindi	English	Hindi
Almonds	Badam	Cinnamon	Dalchini
Asafoetida	Hing	Cloves	Laung
Baby potatoes	Chhote aloo	Cluster beans	Guar falli
Basil leaves	Tulsi ke patte	Coconut	Nariyal
Bay leaf	Tej patta	Colocasia	Arbi
Bengal gram, green	Hara chana	Coriander seeds	Sabut dhania
Bengal gram, split	Chana dal	Corn kernels	Makai ke dane
Bitter gourd	Karela	Cornmeal	Makai ka atta
Black cardamoms	Badi elaichi	Cottage cheese	Paneer
Black gram, skinless split	Dhuli urad dal	Cucumber	Kakdi/kheera
Black gram, split with skin	Chilkewali urad dal	Cudpahnuts	Chironji
		Cumin seeds	Jeera
Black peppercorns	Kali mirch	Dried fenugreek leaves	Kasoori methi
Black salt	Kala namak	Dried mango powder	Amchur
Bottle gourd	Lauki/doodhi	Dried pomegranate seeds	Anardana
Brown Bengal gram	Kala chana	Dried whole red chillies	Sookhi lal mirch
Butter	Makkhan	Dried white peas	Sukhehue safed matar
Button mushrooms	Khumbh/dhingri		
Cabbage	Pattagobhi/ bandhgobhi	Edible silver foil	Chandi ka varq
		Fennel seeds	Saunf
Capsicum	Shimla mirch	Fenugreek leaves	Methi ke patte
Caraway seeds	Shahi jeera	Fenugreek seeds	Methi dana
Carom seeds	Ajwain	Fig	Anjeer
Cashew nuts	Kaju	French beans	Farsi
Cauliflower	Phoolgobhi	Fresh coriander leaves	Taza hara dhania
Chicken	Murgh	Fresh cream	Tazi malai
Chickpeas	Kabuli chane/ chole	Fresh mint leaves	Taze pudine ke patte

English	Hindi	English	Hindi
Fresh spinach leaves	Taza palak	Pomfret	Saranga
Gram flour	Besan	Poppy seeds	Khuskhus
Grapes	Angoor	Prawns/shrimps	Jheenge
Green cardamoms	Chhoti elaichi	Raisins	Kishmish
Green chilli	Hari mirch	Red lentils	Masoor
Green gram	Moong	Red pumpkin	Lal kaddu
Green peas	Hare matar	Refined flour	Maida
Honey	Shahad	Rock salt	Sendha namak
Indian gooseberry	Amla	Rose petals	Gulab ki pankhudiyan
Indian salmon	Rawas		
Jaggery	Gur	Rose water	Gulab jal
Lamb trotters	Paya	Saffron	Kesar
Lemon	Nimboo	Screw pine essence	Kewra
Lemongrass	Hari chai ki patti	Semolina	Sooji/rawa
Melon seeds	Tarbooj ke beej	Sesame seeds	Til
Mussels	Sipi/shambuk	Shallots	Chhote pyaaz
Mustard seeds	Sarson/rai	Split pigeon peas	Toovar dal/ arhar dal
Mutton	Gosht		
Mutton mince	Keema	Spring onion	Hare pyaaz
Nutmeg	Jaiphal	Star anise	Phool chakri/ badiyan
Olives	Jaitun		
Onion seeds	Kalonji	Sweet lime	Mosambi
Orange	Santra	Tamarind	Imli
Papaya	Papita	Turmeric powder	Haldi powder
Parboiled rice	Ukda chawal	Vinegar	Sirka
Parsley	Ajmod	Walnuts	Akhrot
Peanuts	Moongphali	White sesame seeds	Safed til
Pinenuts	Chilgoza	Whole-wheat flour	Atta
Pomegranate kernels	Anar ke dane	Yogurt	Dahi